HOLLYBURN:
THE MOUNTAIN & THE CITY

HOLLYBURN

THE MOUNTAIN & THE CITY

For Hugh & Vivian

Francis Mansbridge

WITH RESEARCH ASSOCIATE, LOIS ENNS

Don Grant

RONSDALE PRESS

HOLLYBURN
Copyright © 2008 Francis Mansbridge

RONSDALE PRESS
3350 West 21st Avenue
Vancouver, BC, Canada V6S 1G7
www.ronsdalepress.com

Typesetting: Julie Cochrane, in Granjon 11.5 pt on 15
Cover Design: Julie Cochrane
Cover Photo: Don Grant
Paper: Ancient Forest Friendly "Silva"–FSC: 100% post-consumer waste, totally
    chlorine-free and acid-free

Ronsdale Press wishes to thank the following for their support of its publishing program: the Canada Council for the Arts, the Government of Canada through the Book Publishing Industry Development Program (BPIDP), and the Province of British Columbia through the Book Publishing Tax Credit program and the British Columbia Arts Council.

Library and Archives Canada Cataloguing in Publication

Mansbridge, Francis, 1943–
    Hollyburn: the mountain & the city / Francis Mansbridge; with Lois Enns.

Includes bibliographical references and index.
ISBN 978-1-55380-062-0

    1. Hollyburn Mountain Region (B.C.)—History. I. Enns, Lois II. Title.

FC3845.H58M35 2008   971.1'33   C2008-905901-8

At Ronsdale Press we are committed to protecting the environment. To this end we are working with Markets Initiative (www.oldgrowthfree.com) and printers to phase out our use of paper produced from ancient forests. This book is one step towards that goal.

Printed in Canada by Marquis Book Printing, Montreal

To the pioneers of Hollyburn,
who created a place of enduring value
which remains for all to enjoy

Contents

Acknowledgements

THIS BOOK COULD NOT have happened without the work and support of many people who believe in Hollyburn's importance. The Hollyburn Heritage Society through Don Grant, Gordon and Iola Knight and Bob and Greta Tapp offered me the opportunity to write this book, giving me free and unlimited use of all their materials. These include extensive newspaper clippings, videos, ski club newsletters, reports, reminiscences and other materials.

Special mention must be made of Don Grant, whose prodigious efforts in interviewing Hollyburners, painstakingly combing through newspapers and gathering research materials have done much to facilitate this project. The selection of photographs for the book has been mainly his work. Collection of oral histories and photographs have been made possible by grants from the District of West Vancouver Arts and Culture Community Grants program, the British Columbia Heritage Trust, the West Vancouver Community Foundation, Helly Hansen through the Alpine Club of Canada and Dayton & Knight Ltd., Consulting Engineers. A portion of the royalties of the book will be donated to the Hollyburn Heritage Society (HHS).

Photographs have been acquired from a number of sources, as indicated. Those identified as "collections" have been acquired by Don Grant of the Hollyburn Heritage Society from various individuals and families. Most of these have been donated to West Vancouver Archives, with electronic copies retained by the Hollyburn Heritage Society.

Thanks to those who read and made helpful comments on the manuscript. These include Don Grant, Gordon and Iola Knight, Bob Tapp and Katharine Steig.

Catherine Rockandel of the Hollyburn Ridge Association loaned me valuable records of their organization, and also helped to clarify many points concerning the cabins and their history. Thanks also to Hugh Johnstone for helpful information on early logging and flumes. Terry Taylor and David Cooke provided valuable information on the natural history of the North Shore mountains, as did Glenn Woodsworth on its geological history. A special thanks to Lois Enns, whose diligent research provided material that has strengthened much of the narrative, especially the non-skiing portion of the book.

Hollyburners interviewed by Don Grant, Iola Knight and Francis Mansbridge include Fred Burfield, Peggy Burfield, Les Finta, Jack Roocroft, Brian Creer, Bob Forrest, Norm Deacon, Barry Deacon, Jacqueline Baker, Bert Brink, Gerry Hardman, Bob Tapp, Jack Rockandel, Don Nelsen, Margaret Ommundsen, Joanne Van Antwerp, Margaret O'Sullivan, Jim Harman, George Bury, Art "Snefty" Senft, Alex Swanson, Jack Wood, Ron Glover, Jim Graham, Laine Loo and Peggy Pratt. These were extremely helpful both for the information supplied and their ability to communicate some of the flavour of earlier times.

For information on the Cypress ski area and related subjects, I am indebted to Wayne Booth, former owner and manager; Linda Swain, current manager; Bobby Swain, operations manager and Bill Cooper, cross-country area manager. Also helpful were Colin Boyd, president of Cypress Ski Club; Alan Bardsley and Bryan Swan of the North Shore Mountain Bike Association; Gerry Brewer of North Shore Rescue; Bill McCuaig and Corinne Ambor of the District of West Vancouver; Andrew Pottinger of British Pacific Properties; Dave Barrett, former British Columbia NDP premier; John Paone, chair of the organizing committee for the freestyle World Cup at Cypress; and Ken Farquharson and Katharine Steig of Friends of Cypress.

The Hollyburn Heritage Society thanks the District of West Vancouver for their continued support.

Thanks most of all to Ronald Hatch, publisher and editor, who combined his personal knowledge of Hollyburn with a meticulous attention to detail and a patient understanding of how the book was developing.

Hollyburn's Cornucopia

*Why are there trees I never walk under but large
and melodious thoughts descend upon me.*

—WALT WHITMAN'S
"SONG OF THE OPEN ROAD"

The Hollyburn cross-country parking lot is almost empty on a late September afternoon. A pair of grouse eye me curiously as I get out of my car, no doubt gauging the possibilities of a handout. As I trudge up the trail a jay precedes me, flitting from stump to stump. Periodically I pass a cabin, mostly shrouded behind the lush vegetation. A half-hour drive from downtown Vancouver, Hollyburn possesses a peace and tranquility that are virtually absolute.

Hollyburn is the mostly forested area lying north of West Vancouver above the 1,200-foot level between Capilano River and Cypress Creek, an area whose gentle slopes make it much more accessible than the other North Shore mountains. It is both the backyard for over two million residents of the Greater Vancouver area and a treasure house of scenic beauty and natural diversity that has few equals anywhere. Nature bursts forth in profusion, its exuberance impelled by plentiful precipitation and a temperate climate.

Along with its neighbours Mount Strachan (pronounced Strahn) and Black Mountain, Hollyburn Mountain is at the southern end of the Coast Mountains of North America. The ancestors of these mountains were created with the subduction of the

Hollyburn Ridge rises above the fledgling community of West Vancouver, ca. 1920s.
(WEST VANCOUVER MEMORIAL LIBRARY 1817)

Farallon and Kula plates under the continental North American plate 80 to 150 million years ago. The compression that built these mountains ceased 45 million years ago, with the formation of one of the largest masses of granitic rock in the world. For the next 40 million years they were quiet, gradually eroding down to a low chain of hills.

Beginning five million years ago, the steepening subduction zone of the Juan de Fuca and Explorer plates caused local melting beneath western BC and Washington. The resulting expansion led to a two kilometre or more uplift, forming the present day Coast Mountains. These mountains continue to rise today.

Glaciation began about two million years ago, with the Cordilleran ice sheet reaching its maximum thickness in the last ice age about sixteen thousand years ago. Glaciation deepened valleys, straightened bends and made the valleys U-shaped rather than V-shaped, which made transportation easier for the incoming human inhabitants. Much of the younger rock has been eroded away, exhuming the range's granitic basement. While mostly granitic, Hollyburn Mountain and Mount Strachan retain roof pendants of older sedimentary rock.

Ice sheets covered the Coast Mountains during the last ice age, with only higher peaks above about 5,500 feet (1,676 metres) protruding. Moving ice and the rock and debris under the glaciers scoured and moulded the lower slopes and ridges, creating

Alex Swanson on the north summit of Unnecessary Mountain, August 1963.
The twin peaks of the Lions are in the background. (ALEX SWANSON COLLECTION)

relatively gradual inclines. The ice disappeared about eleven thousand years ago, melting in the higher areas before the Fraser Valley because the rocks exposed by the melting ice absorbed the heat. The retreating glaciers deposited erratics, large boulders picked up by the glaciers on their slow slide to the sea. Stranded on places such as the top of Mount Strachan and Yew Lake meadows, erratics can still be seen today.

Twelve thousand years ago, when the ice was retreating, a colder and drier climate favoured different trees from today. Lodgepole pine were the first trees to occupy the Hollyburn area after the glaciers, to be followed by Douglas fir and spruce. These were in turn largely supplanted by western hemlock and cedar. In the last 4,000 years cool summers and moist winters have provided the conditions for our present forests.

Temperatures now are moderate and precipitation plentiful. Measured at the Hollyburn Climatological Station at 930 metres, the average precipitation between 1954 and 1990 was 292 centimetres, of which 28 percent fell as snow, with the highest precipitation occurring between October and February. The average April 1st snow depth at Hollyburn is 380 centimetres. Measured during the same period, average daily minimums (in Celsius) ranged from -4.5 degrees in January to 8.1 degrees in August. Daily maximums ranged from 0.7 degrees in December to 17.9 degrees in July and August.

As the largest and oldest living entities with which most of us have any connection, trees occupy a unique space in our imaginations. They are a link to the past and the harbingers of promises for the future. Nurtured by the moist, temperate climate, many of the trees on the west coast have grown to astounding proportions. Some of them were so big that in early days of European settlement individuals—and even families—were said to have used the stumps as floors on which to construct their dwellings.

Up to 300 metres, the Coastal Hemlock Zone is treed with western hemlock, red cedar, Douglas fir, grand fir and yew. Above this level, the Mountain Hemlock Zone is home to mountain hemlock, yellow cedar and amabilis fir (balsam). Conifers dominate both zones because they do better in the dry summers and can grow year-round, competing successfully with the deciduous trees, whose growth is restricted to the summer months.

Yellow and red cedar have played an especially important role in the history of Hollyburn and the lower slopes. The earliest evidence of human presence on Hollyburn occurs on a yellow cedar with bark stripping scars, located above Yew Lake, which may indicate human modification from about 350 to 400 years ago. First Nations people often did not fall trees, but would strip bark or split boards from living trees. Western red cedar was so important to the aboriginal people that they called it the "tree of life." Some said the power of the red cedar was so strong a person could absorb strength by standing with his/her back to the tree. The geographic extent of the northwest coast peoples is about the same as the range of western red cedar, which was crucial to the former's development—it was uncommon until about four thousand years ago.

Cypress Provincial Park is home to some accessible old growth of remarkable size. While many of these trees are very old, it should be pointed out that at this elevation many old trees are not big. A 6.5 to 7.5 inch (16.5 to 19 centimetre) diameter tree cut for a toboggan run checked in at 280 years old. While many have ended up as somebody's shingled roof, 40 percent of the old growth (over two hundred years old) in Cypress Provincial Park remains, with yellow cedar, amabilis fir and mountain and western hemlock the predominant species. It appears that until European presence caused some major fires and environmental changes, no major fire had taken place here for 1,500 to 2,000 years, and possibly as long as 4,700 years, allowing natural development over millennia.

A century of industry by loggers has destroyed most of the great giants of the past, but some of the oldest and largest remaining trees still call Hollyburn-Cypress home. Not long ago a tree eliminated in the interests of a Cypress ski area parking lot was found to be 941 years old. Yellow cedar lives the longest because its wood contains antifungal chemicals that prevent decay. The 1,200-year-old yellow cedar at the Hollyburn Ridge turn-off on the Cypress Bowl Road is, at 2.28 metres in diameter, one of the largest in the Pacific Northwest. Another yellow cedar, named the Hollyburn Giant, is, at 3.2 metres in diameter, even larger, although it is broken-topped and only 20.7 metres high. This tree is located at the junction of the Baden-Powell trail and the old Strachan trail.

Just upslope from the Hollyburn Giant is a mountain hemlock with the largest recorded diameter of any tree of this species in Canada (1.9 metres). The largest known living amabilis, or Pacific silver fir, in the world was discovered in the mid-1980s by famed big tree hunter, the late Randy Stoltmann, near Cabin Lake on Black Mountain. Western hemlock up to 1.8 metres in diameter also flourish on Cypress, including a grove along the Yew Lake old growth trail. Many of these trees have been discovered only recently, and it is possible that even larger specimens may exist in more remote areas visited less by people.

Its magnificent physical setting has helped make Hollyburn home to one of the most popular cross-country ski areas in North America, while the downhill ski area of Cypress next door is being catapulted into the twenty-first century by the upcoming Winter Olympics. Up to 12,000 visitors now come to play in the snow on a busy day, and with the new lifts and infrastructure being completed for the Olympics, that number will grow. The Olympic events of freestyle and aerial skiing at Cypress will confirm Cypress/Hollyburn as the North Shore's premiere locale for winter sports.

Hollyburn's rich and diverse history provides a perspective on many of our changing attitudes to our natural landscape. A variety of sometimes conflicting interests has woven a texture of personalities and events that provide a window into past issues that have shaped our present. From the time that Europeans first settled this area less than a century and a half ago, successive waves of people have etched lineaments on the landscape on both physical and deeper levels. From the increasing urban presence down below, diverse groups have brought their interests up the mountain.

Entrepreneurs, nature lovers and others have found much to attract them to Hollyburn. From 1870, when Sewell Moody hewed his first logging road through the dense forest, commercial interests have been alive to the challenges of the terrain and its lucrative possibilities. Logging roads often became access routes for hikers and skiers—many of whom combined their love of the outdoors with modest commercial activity themselves. The Hollyburn lodge in the cross-country area remains as the only surviving original lodge on the North Shore. Its fate—preservation, renovation

Hikers on the peak of Hollyburn, ca. 1927.
(GEORGE ARMSTRONG-HILLS COLLECTION)

or destruction—is one of the pivotal debates focusing on this area today. Other lodges and establishments such as West Lake/Westlake and Hi-View have provided venues where outdoors enthusiasts have gathered to form bonds that have often lasted generations.

Many Hollyburn skiers, particularly ski jumpers, competed with the world's best in the first half of this century. After the demise of the first chairlift, the development of lift-serviced skiing at Cypress opened a new era—but not without some major environmental struggles, as the lure of the logging dollar led to some ugly and unnecessary clear-cuts. More recent visitors have included mountain bikers, who have developed this area into one of the most highly regarded mountain biking venues anywhere.

Hollyburn also remains home to the only surviving cabin community of the Vancouver area. Many of these rustic retreats, built by early skiers, date back to the early years of this century. They survive as important examples of our built heritage, a link to a time when life was simpler—if harder.

The present state of relatively secure environmental protection belies the colourful and often troubled history of this area. Its proximity to a large urban centre has often placed it under extreme pressure from those with agendas less friendly to the environment. A sense of urgency has characterized many conflicts, as many of the enterprises have had, and will have, permanent effects. The mountain and the city, our natural roots and our urban accomplishments, express the polarities of our modern life. Over the past century these have played out on Hollyburn in various scenarios as loggers, skiers, bikers, developers, environmentalists and others have vigorously promoted their diverse interests. The resulting history provides a fascinating account of some remarkable personalities, a significant part of who we were.

CHAPTER 1

Logging the Slopes

It was an area of primeval forest, untouched by axe or fire.
The timber was western red cedar, western cypress or yellow cedar,
western hemlock, amabilis fir and western white pine. . . .
In these woods you are conscious of a solitude as complete and
primitive as that of the most remote and desolate part of the earth.

—POLLOUGH POGUE

Some said that the trees on the West Coast were so tall that it took two days to see their tops. When felled they took so long to hit the ground that you could go eat dinner and come back to see them still falling. Certainly the trees in the Hollyburn area were an incredible resource which, in the days when wood was king, attracted numerous entrepreneurs. In the second half of the nineteenth century, many buildings and most ships were still made of wood, and few places could boast such excellent timber so close to the water and excellent port and rail facilities. In 1875 geologist and naturalist George Dawson was one of the first to sing the praises of the forest above West Vancouver. He describes these as

truly magnificent woods. Chiefly of Douglas-fir, but also gigantic cedars, & under-growth of vine maple etc. Lichens & moss hanging yards long from lower branches & long straight clean trunks of the Douglas firs stretching up fifty or a hundred feet without a branch. The age of the larger pines is very great often I think over 400 or 500 years.

Logging technology in its early years in this area (beginning about 1870) had a difficult time subduing these mountain giants. Man and axe against a tree ten feet or more in diameter was a major struggle. The early logging companies relied on hard work and ingenuity, and while a few made fortunes, the majority saw most of their profits eaten up by endless expenses. Unreliable water flow in the creeks during Vancouver's dry summers was a perennial problem, as were the deep snows of winter. But other men were always ready to step forward to take up the battle, no doubt in large part attracted by the challenges.

Logging has been the mainstay of BC's economy, providing much of the capital for its development. Loggers opened up the woods, building roads and trails that facilitated access for settlers and recreational users. But loggers also left huge amounts of debris, which provided the fuel for frequent fires that destroyed a great deal of timber and left ugly scars that lasted for generations. Until time and second growth healed the wounds, clear-cuts remained as open sores, confronting present society with its past excesses.

The marquee wood on the North Shore was western red cedar. The largest cedar anywhere, in Canada it grows only in coastal British Columbia. Most felled red cedar ended up as shingles and shakes on roofs and walls throughout North America and beyond, but it was also valued for making doors and door sashes, windows, furniture and coffins. This is one of the lightest of all commercial softwoods. It is straight grained, free of pitch and highly resistant to decay and insect attack. No other wood has cedar's varied colour and texture, and its low shrinkage factor increases the life of cedar-clad roofs and sidewalls. It also provides excellent insulation.

Early logging operations relied on strong backs and axes, three-and-a-half pounds of steel on a three-and-a-half-foot hickory handle, with teams of oxen dragging logs to a mill over roughly constructed skid roads. Since oxen could not handle the steeper slopes, operations started with the most accessible timber near the waterfront, and gradually moved up the mountain to harvest the less accessible. Later, horses expanded the range of possibilities, and flumes were built to transport timber bolts from far up the mountain. Some ingeniously constructed railways and related equipment also enabled the transport of large logs.

Sewell Moody combined a paternal and perhaps self-interested concern for his employees' sobriety and personal well-being with a relentless drive that led to great success before his untimely death in an 1875 shipwreck. Moodyville Sawmill Company's main mill, a little west of the North Vancouver end of the present Ironworkers Memorial Bridge, which had been established in 1863, was running out of easily accessible timber in this area by 1870. That year they received a number of new timber leases, including two in what is now West Vancouver. One was at the mouth of Cypress Creek, about eight hundred metres in depth and extending west towards Point Atkinson, but attempts by Moody to float yellow cedar down the creek were unsuccessful. His main lease, much of which is now British Pacific Properties, stretched west from Capilano River to what is now 22nd Street, going back nearly five miles over the crest of the Ridge. In the early 1860s a fire had killed most of the timber on the lower slopes up to about the 460-metre level, but the standing dead cedars were still valuable timber. A logging camp was set up on today's Ambleside Beach, and Moody became the first to log in West Vancouver. George Dawson describes the camp and area:

> A large stable erected for oxen & mules, & houses for the men. These on the bank above the shore. Lumbering roads radiating back into the woods for several miles. Roads well made, & wide, bankes often cut through & ravines bridged to get greater uniformity of grade. Cross pieces embedded in the road at intervals, & notched in the centre. Oxen tackled to log, which rests on the Cross pieces, man going before team and smearing them with dog-fish oil to make the logs run easily. Trees when felled first deprived of bark by chopping. Then sawn into lengths by hand saw.

Teams of as many as seven pairs of oxen brought the logs to the mill site. In addition, Moody's company began a logging railway to access the steeper terrain the oxen could not handle. Although a trail was graded, and ties and flat cars acquired, rails were never laid. The main camp at Ambleside Beach was abandoned by about 1890, at the end of their standard twenty-one year lease, although the large barn remained standing until 1904. The upper limit of the logging was probably around Elveden Road, where the slopes of Hollyburn Ridge steepened. The last vestiges of the skid roads in the British Properties disappeared in about 1934; Lower Keith Road follows the alignment of one of these from Marine Drive to Esquimalt Avenue. Moody never logged most of the upper part of his Capilano lease.

An increased local market and developing machinery led to a number of companies taking up the North Shore logging challenge in the early years of the twentieth century. The McNair brothers—James, David, Nathaniel, Robert and William—incorporated the McNair Timber Company in August 1906, with their timber lease located west of the Capilano on Moody's old lease. The rapid growth in Canada's population had led to a huge demand in shingles, and the local red cedar, with its resistance to decay, was ideal for this purpose. The McNairs set up a railway log dump and booming ground at the foot of 16th Street, and constructed a railway to facilitate the transportation of logs from higher, steeper terrain. This was also the first company in West Vancouver to use "ground lead" logging, the removal of logs by dragging them out with steam donkeys rather than by animal power.

A much-heralded Heisler steam locomotive arrived in 1907. The plan was to use the friction of the logs it pulled down the planked centre section of the roadbed as a way of braking its speed over the steeper sections of the logging roads. The idea seemed sound, but the absence of restraining logs on its trial run resulted in rapid acceleration that caused it to leap the tracks and become West Vancouver's first train wreck. The company, reorganized as the McNair-Fraser Timber Company, found a replacement in the Walking Dudley, the first machine of its kind in BC, supposedly named for a logger who walked from camp to camp. This 38-ton machine, which arrived in 1908, pulled itself along the rails by means of a grip wheel which engaged fixed cables located on each side of the track. George Smith recalls that they "put a big log on the front and took another right up against it and another one right up against that with some slack in the chain in between so that when they started the front one, it got going fast enough so that it jerked the next one and it started the next one and the next one." As many as sixteen to twenty logs, debarked on one side so that they would slide better, could be moved at a time. By 1909–10, its most profitable year, the company was processing a million feet of logs a month and employing forty-five men.

F. King & W. Allen of Bellingham took over McNair's leases in 1914. As they could not obtain the right-of-way for a flume or the water rights to dam the creeks and divert water, they sold these rights in 1916 to Robert Shields of Vedder River Shingle Co., a "big, jovial energetic man who was very popular in the community." One hundred million feet of cedar suitable for shingles and siding still remained available. Shields' was a shingle operation exclusively, cutting only red cedar. The District of West Vancouver granted him a ten-foot right-of-way and tax reduction on land in return for jobs, providing that he employ "white labour where possible."

In the winter of 1916–17 Shields built a shingle mill on eight acres north of Inglewood, with the office and camp on the west side of Lawson Creek, and the mill buildings on the east side about eight hundred metres north of the Hollyburn ferry landing. Operations started in about February 1917. They also purchased the Canyon Shingle Mill about a mile to the east, which was operated by Johnson & Greene.

In the beginning, horse-drawn sleds transported the bolts to a flume, which carried them down to the mill. Shingle bolts, the raw material from which shingles were split, were fifty-six inches long and the girth of a well-built man. They were split into wedge-shaped sections from a block sawn from a log. To facilitate transport from the rugged slopes, where roads were still a developer's dream, water was diverted from creeks into V-shaped flumes that transported these bolts to a mill. Built from boards milled from local trees, flumes were ingenious—if labour intensive and often inefficient—ways of bringing shingle bolts to more accessible areas. A dam on Lawson Creek at Inglewood Avenue created a pond just south of the mill to receive flumed shingle bolts; from here horses and wagons transported them to the rail station at 14th Street and Bellevue Avenue.

The loggers were continually moving farther up the mountain in pursuit of good wood. In 1917 a second dam higher up on Lawson Creek near the 370-metre level was connected to the lower pond by a two-kilometre flume. Since water was essential to "grease" the flumes, a box flume was built westward across the mountain in 1918 to bring water from Cypress Creek from the 366-metre level to the 304-metre level. The amount of work that went into the building of these flumes is now hard to believe, and in this case the box-shaped flume carried no wood at all, simply water for the V-flumes that carried the shingle bolts.

In spite of this huge effort, the water supply was still unreliable. Shields built a light-rail narrow-gauge tramway in the early twenties adjacent to the flume from the mill to the upper pond. Three steam donkeys lowered the loaded cars successively to the lower mill pond two kilometres below. A second tramway was later built northeastward to the 630-metre level near the watershed boundary. Pollough Pogue describes this early railway "extending into virgin timber, a magnificent forest of dark-green scented cedar, many of the trees ten feet or more at the butt, and of an age surpassing belief."

The high point of production for the Shields operation came just after the Japanese earthquake of 1923, which triggered an increased demand for shingles. The Shields mill had a reputed capacity of 360,000 shingles a day, with as many as seven-

Hikers at the box flume dam on Cypress Creek, ca. 1930. L to R: Con Brown, Tom Elsdon and Lorne Elsdon. (SCOTTY FINLAYSON COLLECTION)

West Vancouver and Hollyburn Ridge, ca. 1930, showing the approximate route of Shields' box flume, and the V-flume and tramway for transporting shingle bolts to Inglewood Mill.

(WEST VANCOUVER ARCHIVES. RUPERT HARRISON COLLECTION. 0362.WVA.RAH PHOTOGRAPH BY PACIFIC AIRWAYS LTD.)

ty-five to ninety men employed. The company operated until mid-1926 when they exhausted the profitable timber in their lease. The mill was dismantled and the machinery removed in the spring of 1927.

The skid roads and trails remained to form the basis for the original main trail from the top of 15th Street to old West Lake and Lost Lake. A good trail alongside the Shields box flume—from the sorting pond on Lawson Creek at Millstream Road to the reservoir on Cypress Creek—also provided mountain access. The flumes disappeared in the late 1940s when holdings of the British Pacific Properties were clear-cut from Glenmore to Horseshoe Bay to the 400-metre level, although the tramway can still be traced from the Millstream Pond to the skyline site.

In 1913 Thomas Cardinell had opened a small shingle mill west of 27th Street on the north side of the PGE (Pacific Great Eastern) line where he manufactured twenty-four-inch shingles. He sold this company to the Ritchie brothers, who formed the Cypress Lumber Company in 1916. They acquired six square miles of leases above the 660-metre level and built a 1,190-metre dry chute from the claim to a pond on Rodgers Creek above Marine Drive. From here horses and wagons took the logs to the mill. This chute was another idea that sounded better than it was. One report stated that the "bolts travelled so fast down the steep incline that, after covering about one-fourth of the trip, many of them jumped the chute, rose forty feet or so in the air, and landed in the gulch far below." This was changed to a 3,000-metre wet flume using water from Rodgers and Marr creeks that worked better, although insufficient water for full-time operation limited its use and the company's profitability. The mill closed in the fall of 1917.

All this industrial activity was no doubt very good for the economy, but not everyone was applauding. Provincial botanist John Davidson in his perceptive paper "The

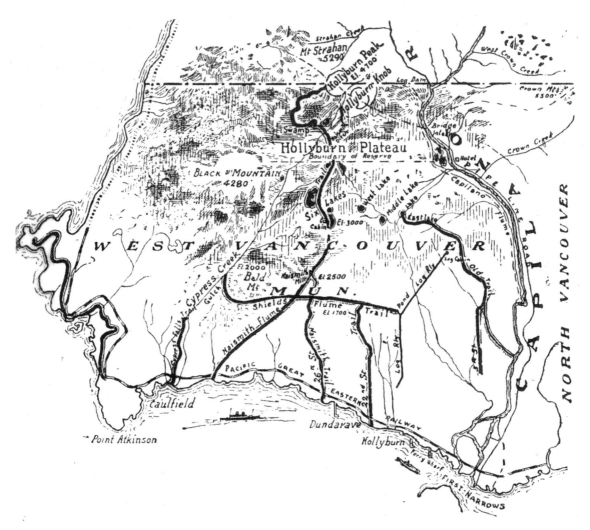

Flumes and trails in early logging, 1925. (DAILY PROVINCE)

Hikers on a Hollyburn Ridge flume, early 1920s.
(WEST VANCOUVER ARCHIVES. JACK CRUICKSHANK FONDS. 017.WVA.CRU)

Hand-writing on the Wall," given October 1, 1924, to the Vancouver Natural History Society, decried the devastation that logging companies who "steal the heritage of future generations" have inflicted on our environment. He describes how

> A few years ago a company started a mill on Hollyburn Ridge, part of which drains into Cypress Creek. Ask the residents of Cypress park what the result was. The Spring freshets turned the otherwise beautiful creek into a roaring, rushing, turbulent torrent, breaking its banks, washing out roads and paths and depositing a deep layer of sand and gravel over the lawns and gardens of residents who had spent much time and money in beautifying their homes.

The mill referred to here is probably Nasmyth's mill (often given different spellings), whose upper mill buildings became headquarters for the first commercial ski operation on the North Shore mountains. While logging's economic benefits fuelled the growth of the community and opened up the forests to other users, some of the recreational users agreed with Hollyburn's chronicler Pollough Pogue. "When a tree is cut down, I suffer in spirit with it. I suppose I am really a sort of druid."

In July 1918, James H. Nasmyth purchased the holdings of the Cypress Lumber Company, including their six square miles of leases and shingle mill at Dundarave. Nasmyth dismantled a sawmill from Burnaby and moved it on skids pulled by a

Hikers resting at the abandoned Nasmyth Mill, 1925.
(TED AND ELSIE WORTHINGTON COLLECTION)

steam donkey engine via a tote road from 26th Street and Palmerston Avenue in West Vancouver to the 760-metre level in West Vancouver. With this move he became the first to log above the 600-metre level.

Nasmyth had a total of five leases in the Cypress Creek Valley, including land on both Hollyburn and Black Mountain. Realizing the importance of water for logging operations, he applied for and received "four cubic feet" of water per second to be taken from Cypress Creek to flume shingle bolts and lumber to tidewater, and to store "400 acre feet" of water out of Cypress Creek. Some intricate and laborious engineering then took place. First Lake was dammed, and Third, Fourth and Fifth lakes were enlarged, using small dykes of mud, sticks and stone. Drainage ditches were built connecting Sixth, Third and Fourth lakes to ensure an adequate supply of water to the main reservoir in First Lake. Water was released from First Lake into a box flume that followed the west bank of Marr Creek to a point near Burn-a-Bee cabin. Here it crossed the main trail to merge with Rodgers Creek, then to the holding pond at the mill. This water then augmented the water flow needed for the transportation of shingle bolts in Nasmyth's flume to tidewater. Early resident George Smith recalls the thrills of riding the flume as a young boy. "And it was dangerous as hell, because some places [were] thirty or forty feet off the ground."

The building of flumes and drainage ditches necessitated numerous trails to bring supplies to the mill. Skid roads from the head of 22nd, 25th and 26th streets converged just below the mill site to form one road at a point that was later called

"The Forks." These roads would soon become access routes for hikers and skiers.

Nasmyth improved the old Cypress flume, which supplied shingle bolts to the 27th Street mill. A new 3.6-kilometre flume transported cut lumber from the upper mill to a planing mill and shipping platform at Sherman station on the Pacific Great Eastern Railway. Because sawn lumber moved poorly down the flume, Nasmyth concentrated on shingle bolts. At best this was a marginal operation, with lack of water, long winter shutdowns and the high cost of removing the timber limiting their success. Nasmyth shut down in late 1923, with the abandoned upper mill soon becoming the initial site of the Hollyburn Ski Camp; the lumber salvaged from the flumes was a great source for cabin-building materials.

The companies discussed so far were the major players in early logging. There were also, however, many small "haywire" or "gyppo" operations which came and went, often leaving behind disgruntled loggers looking for a paycheque. But by 1928, most of the best and most accessible timber had been already taken out, and from 1928 to 1946 only small outfits operated, with independent loggers working the slopes using horses or small steam or gasoline donkeys. Names include Seymour, Lacy, the Reynolds brothers, Jack Summerfield and Frank Corbett. From 1940 to 1970 logging enterprises once more became extensive, and, as will be seen, some major conflicts between developers and conservationists defined the direction Hollyburn would take.

CHAPTER 2

Early Days of Recreation: Discovering Hollyburn's Spirit

*To once behold the alpine loveliness of Hollyburn
is to fall under its spell, and if a hiker once climbs the
great ridge he will climb it again and again.*

—POLLOUGH POGUE

While today Hollyburn refers to the cross-country skiing/hiking area on the upper part of the mountain, the name originally referred to a location in West Vancouver. The *Vancouver Daily Province*, December 11, 1946, recounts the origin of the Hollyburn name:

> Mr. Lawson's first trip to Vancouver was in 1890, but it was not until a later trip, 1904 to be exact, that he saw his first holly trees. When the train stopped at Agassiz, he noticed the trees growing in the station grounds. He was so taken with their glossy leaves and bright berries, he decided to get some for himself. In Vancouver, he bought a couple of trees from M.J. Henry Nurseries in Mount Pleasant and planted them in his garden on Pacific Street.
>
> But Mr. Lawson was not settled. He had looked over at the North Shore on his first trip in 1890, and subsequently bought himself some land, a mere 125 acres, all waterfront. Part of this was purchased from Mr. J.C. Keith, manager of the Bank of British North America who had himself bought it from the famous "Navvy Jack."
>
> Mr. Lawson built his first home at what is now Seventeenth St. and waterfront

and here he planted his two trees. Sounds like a simple operation to us today, rushing across the bridge when we feel like it. But it was not so simple then. Mr. Lawson hired a rowboat at English Bay, loaded his trees and rowed them over.

Later he set out some cuttings. He was told if he planted some fresh meat with them, it would make them grow better. This he did, but the bears must have heard about it, because they came down one dark night and dug up every one.

...

Mr. Lawson racked his brain for a name for his property. Then he had an inspiration. He had enough Scotch blood to think of his rushing, roaring Mountain creek as a burn. And there were his beautiful holly trees growing along side it. Hence, Hollyburn, and a most happy choice.

Hollyburn remains a popular name for a number of West Vancouver businesses and organizations, but the name first made its way up the mountain with the botanist John Davidson, who named the mountain area Hollyburn on a botanical survey in July 1912. He thought the name fitting, as it was immediately above the Hollyburn Post Office in West Vancouver—and so it has remained to this day, with Hollyburn Mountain replacing the earlier name of Mount Vaughan.

Many who hiked and skied the slopes of Hollyburn in the early days recall a time when youthful energy discovered a cherished oasis, where a community spirit and keen but friendly competition cemented lifelong bonds. From the perspective of a later century, one perceives a spirit of simplicity and untrammelled fun, glistening like a fresh fall of snow in the morning sun. Memories of scenic grandeur mingle with recollections of physical challenge and heartwarming times spent with friends and family.

For many who spent a good part of their early lives on Hollyburn, the pull is deep and lasting. Winifred "Buddy" Oliver (née Barker) started going up Hollyburn as a teenager in 1925. In 1997, when she turned ninety, she "did lots of things for the last time." One was a solo hike from First Lake to the top of Hollyburn Mountain, an elevation gain of over 425 metres. (She turned 101 in 2008.) Her friend Gerry Hardman was one of several who hiked Hollyburn well into his eighties. As Geordie Tocher says, it's "part of my blood." Joan Greaves (née Whitney) recalls that

> . . . if I ever get into a situation where I want to feel really calm, I think about the climb from the top of the shoulder. There were always these beautiful trees that were weighted down with snow. We never stayed long, but I always thought it was one of the most physically beautiful places to see.

Jewel lakes and rolling hills combine with heather-dotted glades. Views of Vancouver and beyond are spectacular, with the snowy dome of Mount Baker an almost palpable presence on clear days. Wisps of grey cloud often drift in from the ocean, softening and shrouding the landscape, imbuing it with a mystical, unearthly atmosphere. Northward the mountains rise in endless snowy tiers.

Naomi Wilson MacInnes and Hugh "Torchy" Aikens, on the Hollyburn shoulder, ca. 1940.
(JACK AND PEGGY PRATT COLLECTION)

Writing in 1976, Naomi MacInnes recalls, "Those were a few magic years in my lifetime, a never-to-be-forgotten period in my growing up that made a lasting impression on me and actually shaped my future." Peggy Burfield, whose parents operated Hollyburn Ski Lodge for many years, recalls her childhood there in the 1950s and 1960s with warm nostalgia. Favourite spots on the mountain remain a touchstone for her imagination. Hollyburn, she says, shaped her life, instilling in her the importance of the environment, the value of friendship, and a grounding in basic values.

North Vancouver pioneer and entrepreneur Edward Mahon, whose name is perpetuated in North Vancouver's Mahon Park and Mahon Avenue, built one of the first Hollyburn cabins in about 1895 at East Lake (now Lost Lake) in what is now the southeast corner of Cypress Park. The February 14, 1935, *Hiker and Skier* reports that he cut the first trail across Hollyburn Ridge. The first recorded ascent of Hollyburn Mountain was made in 1908 by a group from the Vancouver Mountaineering Club (later the BC Mountaineering Club). Many trekked to Hollyburn before World War I via Brothers Creek.

The luxuriant diversity of plant life makes this area a botanist's paradise. The most important of the early botanical visitors was John Davidson, who arrived in Canada from Scotland's University of Aberdeen in April 1911. He was soon appointed provincial botanist and hired to conduct a botanical survey of British Columbia.

Buddy Barker (centre right) and Kitty Franklin (centre) at Pollough Pogue's camp on Hollyburn Ridge, May 24, 1925. Pogue is standing on the far right, with his son Mickey behind Kitty Franklin. (WIN OLIVER/BUDDY BARKER COLLECTION)

Hollyburn, already recognized as being vital to British Columbia's ecological diversity, was included in this survey. On July 11, 1912, Davidson set off from North Vancouver with Fred Perry and Bill Taylor to gather information on the flora of Black Mountain. This multi-day excursion was not the simple drive that anyone visiting the area today would make. They crossed Capilano Canyon and proceeded northwest, camping on Hollyburn Ridge at an elevation of 915 metres. The group then followed Cypress Creek to its headwaters and ascended Black Mountain from the northeast slopes, where they camped the second night. After gathering specimens they returned via its southwest slopes to Eagle Lake and camped the next night near Caulfeild.

Scouting had come to Canada in the spring of 1908, and, in the years following, Scout and Cub leaders often took groups up Hollyburn. Bert Brink joined a Cub pack in Kitsilano when he was about eight, and started going up Hollyburn in 1920 with his pack leader Canon Sovereign. Later he studied at the University of British Columbia (UBC) under John Davidson and others, and then took his PhD in genetics and biochemistry at the University of Wisconsin, becoming a professor of agronomy at UBC.

A founder and later president of the Federation of BC Naturalists in 1959, he also organized Vancouver Natural History Society summer camps for nearly fifty years, and was a founding director of The Nature Trust of British Columbia in 1973, spending much of his time on Hollyburn. He was made an officer in the Order of Canada, and a member of the Order of British Columbia. In 2007 he was honoured with the Lieutenant Governor's conservation award for his outstanding contribution towards wetland conservation and education in BC Lieutenant Governor Iona Campognolo described him as "British Columbia's icon of environmental conservation and sustainability." In December 2007 Bert passed away at the age of ninety-five.

Scout troop near Sixth Lake, Hollyburn Ridge, 1920s.
(WEST VANCOUVER ARCHIVES. GEORGE SMITH FAMILY FONDS. 427.WVA.SMI)

Bert was one of the first pioneers of Hollyburn. He made his first pair of skis and, with friends, built a number of cabins. While most cabins were built in the lower part of the skiable area, one cabin Brink helped build was higher up the mountain, above Sixth Lake. He recalls this as difficult, as the wood at this elevation was very tough. When West Vancouver declared this cabin to be within the watershed, and hence not permissible for private use, it became the Romstad's first aid cabin.

Bob Forrest, who served as president of the Hollyburn Pacific Ski Club, first went up Hollyburn about 1920 with a Cub pack led by Mr. Graham. He next visited the area in 1925 at the age of twelve with Bert Brink, where he spent a memorable night in the open behind a log, but did not become a regular Hollyburner until about 1931. For a while he and his friend Don Dewar bunked in with Pollough Pogue in his cabin, but then built their own with Pollough's son Mickey and others. Bob remembers attending the opening of the first West Lake Lodge in 1933, and subsequently enjoyed many dances there—he recalls that he most often took the trail to West Lake from the British Properties. Now well past ninety, he lives in his Vancouver westside bungalow.

Legendary mountaineer Phyllis Munday introduced many young women to hiking and mountaineering on the North Shore through her work as a Guide leader. Guides and Scouts have continued to make significant contributions. Between 1967 and 1971, they built the Baden-Powell trail, a 50-kilometre route that winds precipitously across the North Shore from Horseshoe Bay to Deep Cove. Members of the Varsity Outdoor Club from UBC, founded in November 1917 by Rhodes scholar Dr. Harry V. Warren and others, were also early visitors.

The BC Mountaineering Club newsletter credits the first record of skiing on the North Shore mountains to Phyllis Beltz and her husband in the early years of the century (on Grouse Mountain). Until shortly before her death in 1974 at eighty-two, Phyllis hiked regularly to her cabin on Hollyburn Ridge. Her son, John Beltz, later became engaged in intense environmental struggles in the Hollyburn area.

Of the many colourful individuals whose lives have been entwined with Hollyburn, none is more enigmatic and intriguing than Pollough Pogue. Born Gerald Leslie Marston Pogue in 1875 in Lindsay, Ontario, probably of Irish origin, he arrived in British Columbia in about 1920. Bob Forrest believes that prior to coming to British Columbia, Pogue was a marine editor in Philadelphia, and allusions in his *Province* articles suggest he also lived in Quebec. Pogue soon became an ardent promoter of Hollyburn's splendour:

> To once behold the alpine loveliness of Hollyburn is to fall under its spell and if a
> hiker once climbs a great ridge he will climb again and again. In summertime when
> the huge plateau is overspread with purple and white heather, rhododendron and
> many varieties of mountain wildflowers, and water lilies cover the still surfaces of

Pollough Pogue at the Nasmyth Mill site, late 1920s.
(OMMUND OMMUNDSEN COLLECTION)

the lakes, Hollyburn is the most popular with weekend hikers of all the mountains in the Vancouver district.

Pogue began writing for the *Vancouver Daily Province* in early 1922. Some four hundred articles appearing in this newspaper from 1922 to 1929 provide a romantic, intimate account of his experience of the natural and human life of the North Shore, mostly Hollyburn. These are highly literate, their style owing much to the English Romantic poets, with whom he appears intimately familiar. Pogue added an imaginative dimension to the experience of Hollyburn by bringing to his work an eye for detail and an ability to invest it with personal meaning.

When rising rents forced him out of his home in Altamont in March 1925, he established a camp on Black Mountain at the 460-metre level, using a tent over a platform built from planks salvaged from an old timber flume. When he set up his camp, "There came an unhoped for, hardly believable suffusion of warm light in the western sky. . . . Dripping trees and soaked salal were flooded with gold and shone like a field of paradise. The miasma of sardonic pessimism cleared away from my soul." Here he lived like his American counterpart Henry Thoreau, in close harmony with nature, his tent a place where the local residents were welcomed. "A number of times the playful woodrats tripped nimbly over my face and form as I lay on my starboard side lost in slumber." "Old Bill" was one of these. "'Eat hearty, old boy,' I always tell him. 'I like your company, so come every evening. As long as I've got any grub you are welcome to a meal. I'm a kind of old bushrat myself.'"

The theft of his tent in December left him homeless again. Eilif Haxthow and his friends at the Old Mill camp fixed up a cabin for him at this site. He became the patrol man at the local fire tower in the summer of 1928, and lived thereafter in various cabins on Hollyburn. His devotion to Hollyburn was complete. "If you would like to dwell for a while in a solitude of hemlock, cypress and fir, to recuperate your health, or cure any of the maladies of civilization, you could not go to a better place." Pogue suffered from iritis, an eye inflammation caused by childhood polio, but cured it, he says, by bathing it in a Hollyburn fountain of youth, as he describes in sensuously embroidered Keatsian detail:

> I heard in the deep damp woods behind my camp, the silver reshuffling of a miniature waterfall. It led me to a sweet defile of black moist rocks decorated with patterns of lichen in green and copper impasto. Between these cool and swarthy walls descended a small stream, dropping in creamy showers over dark ledges, falling in veils of snow from ten-foot precipices, collecting in pools darkly green and edged with clotted froth. To one of these pools, beneath a musical cascade, at the bottom of a chasm as dark as a grotto, I resorted with my inflamed iris and bathed it with the pure snow-cold water: almost at once I felt its curative powers.

Florence Brewis describes his presence during the building of the first West Lake Lodge in the early thirties. "I can still see him wearing the ancient woollen toque that he never seemed to remove, the heavy grey logger's shirt open at the neck, showing a glimpse of soiled Stanfields, thick wool pants held up by broad suspenders as well as a wide belt and logger's moccasin style boots."

To curb the destruction done to municipal and private property on Hollyburn by the influx of hikers, Pogue was appointed Special Constable in 1927, but his life was always a struggle. His letter to Reeve J.B. Leyland June 15, 1932, describes both his need for assistance and his work as an unofficial fire prevention officer: "I would be glad if the Council would give me some food, as I had none and was depending on the boys at the ski camp for anything to eat." Leyland agreed that he be paid a nominal ten dollars monthly. "All I ask is that a careful watch should be kept on any hikers who might be guilty of cutting down trees, increasing the fire hazard, or entering private properties, without permission." Pogue moved to a fire tower below the Old Mill site to guard against the perceived (and very real) threat of fire to the North Shore. Later he moved to a cabin near First Lake which became a popular place for passersby to stop for a mug of tea. He left the mountain only to replenish his supplies, supplemented by berries, mushrooms and game found on the mountain. In 1927 he urged setting aside the area as a provincial park to guard it against the twin perils of fire and commercialism.

Pogue maintained an ongoing if distant relationship with his wife in the city below. While she worked with him on the newsletter *Hiker and Skier*, she never went up the mountain. Of their three children, Mickey was especially active as a skier and builder, and Molly also visited the mountain frequently. Pollough died March 28, 1961, in Shawnigan Lake, BC.

A Hollyburner from the next generation, Gerry Hardman is memorialized by a snow post at First Lake, endowed by his heirs and designed and erected in 2004 by the

Gerry Hardman on Black Mountain, September 1930.
(GERRY HARDMAN COLLECTION)

West Vancouver ferry "Hollyburn" coming into Ambleside, June 1937.
(GERRY HARDMAN COLLECTION)

Hollyburn Heritage Society. He moved to West Vancouver with his family in 1920 when he was nine, living in a tent near what is now Earl's Restaurant at 303 Marine Drive. He started going up Hollyburn when he was eleven, often riding down the mountain on shingle bolts on the Nasmyth flume from the Nasmyth Mill site to Sherman Station on the railway tracks. He built three cabins, selling the last one after his wife died. He remained a day hiker into his nineties. He passed away in 2002.

While the earliest visitors were hikers, beginning in the 1920s most of those drawn to Hollyburn were young urbanites making the trek from Vancouver to practise the new sport of skiing, or ski-running, or Norwegian snowshoes, as it was also called. After a week of working for the dollar in downtown stores and offices, the outdoor enthusiasts packed their gear to the foot of Columbia Street, where the *Doncella*, *Sonrisa*, *West Vancouver No. 5*, or *West Vancouver No. 6* ferried them to Ambleside in West Vancouver for the grand price of ten cents. From here the thriftier walked to Marine Drive, then west, cutting through what is now West Vancouver Memorial Park, then along a route scattered with houses to where 22nd Street shaded into an old skid road. Those with extra cash sprang for another nickel for a bus to Mathers Avenue and 22nd Street, some of which had special outside racks for skis and packs. Naomi McInnes recalls the efforts needed to reach Hollyburn before bridges and roads made it all simpler:

I worked at the Bay which closed at 6 p.m. in those days. My pack had been carried with me to the streetcar in the morning, and I changed into hiking clothes in the locker room, then rushed by foot to catch the 7 p.m. ferry. Add to that the 30 minute ferry crossing, bus ride, 2-hour hike and final jaunt to the dance. . . . It has occurred to me that we may have been in such great physical condition from the hiking we did, that injuries were almost impossible to sustain in such a hardy group.

Groceries and supplies could be purchased at Allison's Marine Grocery at 22nd Street and Marine Drive, or, to save some packing, at Jim and Sadie Sambrook's weekend store at the Forks on the trail at the 700-metre level. Here a loaf of home-baked bread cost ten cents, and potatoes two-and-a-half cents a pound. Snacks of coffee and hot dogs were also available.

In the 1940s, Bob Caverley started a coffee shop, joined by Art Senft or, as he was commonly called, Snefty, in 1947. The Old Mill Coffee Shop between the Forks and the Old Mill supplied gas and oil for the cabins as well as hamburgers, hot dogs and chips for the skiers. Snefty also supplied juice cans for "bugs" at a quarter apiece, made by inserting candles through a hole in the side of five-pound jam cans, a main source of light for nighttime travelling. After the December 1941 attack on Pearl Harbor, he helped make covers for flashlights that allowed only a slit of light, supposedly making the area less vulnerable to enemy attack. Until Snefty left for the Queen Charlottes in 1950, the Old Mill Coffee Shop served a little bit of everything—hotcakes, hot dogs, hamburgers and chips—and also sold supplies for cabins. Initially Snefty rented the Valhalla, then with Bill Christie built a unique eight-sided cabin.

Snefty is best known for his rollicking folksy poetry which he often read on Dan Russell's radio show (CJOR). He has written numerous poems, mostly, he says, on sports personalities, with a number published in the *Province*. These are on such diverse figures as Karen Magnussen, Linda Moore, Elizabeth Manley, Gordie Howe, Doug Flutie, Nancy Greene and Helen Kelesi. He has also written a number of poems on Hollyburn, such as the following:

> We leave the city far below
> To visit a heritage lodge
> that we know.
> Many fond memories of years gone by,
> We found in this paradise
> close to the sky.

Another place for buying snacks was farther up the mountain where Ed "Annie" Oakley sold hot dogs at his "Sun Valley Palace" at the foot of Romstad's ski run on good skiing days.

Ed Oakley at his hot dog stand near the foot of Romstad's, ca. 1940.
(CHUCK AND JUNE GILLRIE COLLECTION)

As the early pioneers began to shape Hollyburn, the residential areas below also took shape. While the District of West Vancouver had been incorporated in 1912, it remained mostly rural for some time. Doug Watt, who was born in 1921, describes it as

> a village, really, with limited pockets of development at Ambleside/Hollyburn, Dundarave, and, further out, West Bay, Cypress/Caulfeild and Horseshoe Bay/Whytecliff. Most of the limited number of north/south streets were fringed with deep, open ditches and sidewalks were something we knew about only from occasional trips "over town" (as Vancouver was referred to), except for an elevated (a foot above ground level) wooden sidewalk on the south side of Marine Drive from 14th to 18th streets.

Gradually West Vancouver acquired the infrastructure of a separate town. In 1919 the *West Vancouver Courier*, the district's first newspaper, started publishing, although it closed in 1921. Electric power arrived in 1922, making possible the opening of the Hollyburn Theater in 1926. The Gleneagles Golf Course opened in 1927.

Meanwhile Vancouver flourished as the 1920s progressed. By 1925 it had a population of 126,000, with some 500 industrial operations employing 14,000 people. The Second Narrows Bridge opened the same year, making road access to the North Shore possible for the first time. Percy Williams ignited civic and national pride with his victories in the 100 and 200 yards at the 1928 Amsterdam Olympics. The Denman arena on Georgia Street, seating 10,000, was the world's second artificial ice arena. Large neon signs began to appear. Vancouver was a feisty city imbued with exuberant energy, looking for new challenges and new activities.

A number of trails initially provided access to Hollyburn, including one (long since overgrown) from the west end of Capilano Suspension Bridge. Other routes owed much to earlier logging. There was a logging skid road from the top of 26th Street, but most heading for the Hollyburn Ski Camp area took the trail from the top of 22nd Street, which was not as steep or rough. This route, which took about two hours on good legs, headed up 22nd to Marr Creek, around the side hill following the old box flume built by Shields, then straight up toward the Old Mill on the trail that follows up from 26th Street. For many, this was a portal to a more benign universe. Pogue comments: "As soon as people are on a trail they throw aside the aloofness and arbitrary customs of an artificial civilization. They act as men and women in ages past, when a friendly word was a peace sign, and only enemies passed without a greeting." Here a stream or a creek "abundantly supplied by the dissolving snows above, laughed and flashed beside the decayed skid road; shy birds hidden among the leaves musically whistled: the forest had been revitalized in a damp luxuriance of green growth springing from the ground."

Miner-style carbide lights and flashlights became popular in the 1930s when the Scandinavian miners became a part of mountain life, although Art Senft recalls that as late as 1950 bug lights were still popular, while the carbide lights became less so. As many as 400 skiers made the hike on a winter Friday night, their lights creating a luminous chain linking city and mountain.

CHAPTER 3

The Hollyburn Ski Camp:
"Where Winter Lingers in the Lap of Summer"

*Life in that high place was a superior life, sharper and larger than
life at sea-level. In this white and shining region, the air you breathe
produces an elation of mind and also a physical animation.*

—*HIKER AND SKIER*, JANUARY 30, 1935

Until the early years of the past century, snowshoeing was the traditional
Canadian way of navigating the winter wilderness, conjuring up images of
coureurs du bois in colourful garb singing rousing French-Canadian folk songs. But
once the Scandinavians began arriving, skiing, at this time a new sport in Canada,
and particularly suited to the mountainous terrain of British Columbia, took hold.
Attracted to BC by work in logging and mining, Scandinavians brought with them
both their skis and their philosophy of sport and camaraderie: a spirit of co-operation
in undertaking tasks, and a warm friendliness to all visitors.

While Pollough Pogue chronicled the diversity of Hollyburn's nature and the
early European presence, Rudolph Verne provided much of the push for development. An entrepreneurial Swede with restless energy, Verne combined a passion for
skiing with imagination and practical common sense. He first visited Vancouver in
the spring of 1914, where he was one of the first to ski on Grouse Mountain. On
returning to Alberta he built the first ski hill in Elbow Park, Calgary, where some ten
thousand watched the opening of the jump. In January 1921 he was part of a group

that built the "World's Most Spectacular Ski Jump" as part of Calgary's winter carnival—on the roof of the Calgary Exhibition Grandstand. The apocalyptically named "Hell Dive Ski Chute" attracted approximately fifteen thousand spectators over two days.

Verne returned to Vancouver in 1922 where the Vancouver Connaught Skating Club hired him as their club professional. From his room on West Georgia, views of the snow-capped mountains of the North Shore intrigued him. On the Norwegian national holiday of May 17, 1922, Verne set off with a friend to explore potential ski country on the North Shore. Their intended destination was Grouse Mountain, but boarding the wrong ferry landed them in West Vancouver. As they could see no snow from the 14th Street wharf, they left their skis there and hiked a trail that led them to the vacant Nasmyth Mill buildings, then continued on up to First Lake.

Here, Verne recalls, "I had acquired enough vision to imagine the establishment of a future ski camp." They had lunch and continued to hike to the peak of Hollyburn. In the 1926–27 *Canadian Ski Annual*, Verne recalls:

> We were on an extensive high level plateau, a heavy blanket of snow covering all underbrush to a depth of eight feet, offering the most perfect skiing imaginable, while the stand of Western Cypress with its silver bark added a truly Alpine touch to the winter landscape. In the distance mighty Mount Baker reared his majestic snow-clad head; further south Mount Rainier was plainly visible 189 miles distant, with the crater-like peak of Mt. Garibaldi in the midst of the glacier-filled Garibaldi Park in full view, and close at hand a mountain chain resembling the Canadian Rockies all around 5,000 feet in height. It was a gorgeous outlook, its beauty overwhelming. We had discovered a veritable skier's paradise, eclipsing anything I'd ever seen or mentioned.

Perhaps the luxuriant growth and the gently contoured mountains reminded him of his Scandinavian homeland. The winter after his initial trip to Hollyburn, he organized a ski trip there, charging each participant two dollars (for many, at this time, a day's wages).

Plans for a ski camp soon began, although the use of the Nasmyth cabins by hikers and skiers predates by some years Verne's development of this location. The December 1923 BCMC newsletter, in connection with a proposed trip to Mount Strachan, states that "there is some doubt about being allowed free use of the mill buildings as in the past, owing to an attempt to turn the logging camp for the winter into a stopping place for parties visiting Hollyburn Ridge." Their February 1924 newsletter reassures their membership that "at least one of the mill cabins on Hollyburn seems to be unlocked all the time, and there seems to be no objection to its use by Club members."

Verne opened Vancouver's first ski store in 1923, selling skis that he imported from Hagins of Oslo. He was more visionary and entrepreneur than hands-on builder but found the ideal person to flesh out his Hollyburn dreams in Eilif Haxthow, a young Norwegian who was both handy and energetic. Haxthow had immigrated to Canada from Oslo on the *Blenheim* on August 25, 1923, when only eighteen. After a winter spent as a pulp tester in Timiskaming, and a summer spent wandering and working, mostly on the prairie harvest, he arrived in Vancouver on November 14, 1924. He found it "big enough" and "rather attractive in and of itself" with "lots of amenities." Verne put Haxthow under contract in December 1924 to develop facilities at the abandoned Nasmyth lumber operation at the 760-metre elevation, setting up a business renting skis and selling coffee and sandwiches. With Verne, Haxthow invested all he had in this new undertaking.

Haxthow worked with Hjalmer Fahlander, a Swede, to convert the cookhouse at the old Nasmyth mill site on Rodgers Creek into a ski camp. This was about two hundred metres south of milepost seven (near kilometre ten) at the last switchback on the present Cypress Bowl Road. Vandalism had caused disintegration of the mill, but the two young men, with material from the now abandoned flume, repaired and cleaned the shacks, built new bunks, tables and chairs, and rehabilitated the old stoves.

Life on the mountain in winter was Spartan, with the ski camp boys' meagre diet often augmented by game they could snare or shoot. Haxthow's journal, which he kept in Norwegian from 1923 until 1928, later translated into English by Jorgen Dahlie, renders a vivid account of the pleasures of his day-to-day life. A talented artist, he often created oil paintings on cedar slabs hewn from the slopes of Hollyburn.

"The Restaurant" at the former Nasmyth Mill, 1925.
(EILIF HAXTHOW COLLECTION)

In January 1925, Haxthow and Fahlander opened "The Restaurant," with Eric Ahlberg joining them as a partner in February. For the first time ever, both beginners and committed skiers had a place to go where they could rent skis, buy refreshments, and bond with their fellows—although it took a while for the business to develop. The first weekend's take was a meagre eight dollars but, by the end of January, weekends were bringing in thirty dollars. Haxthow's journal entry for January 11, 1925, a few days after The Restaurant opened for business, is full of hope:

> Now we are going! Now things are moving! For a long time it seemed hopeless. We have had five opening days that were a disaster. But today, Sunday the 11th of January, 1925, we were surprised early in the morning as people streamed in more and more. The restaurant was not ready for such an onslaught but the skis—nine pairs —got used the whole day. Snow made the difference but the Canadians were the heroes.

Skiers, as described by Pogue, ran "from the top of the sawdust bank . . . down the steep narrow road between the cabins and the stumps. When you get to the stable, the lowest of the cabins, or a little distance past it, you must fall."

Dances in the Rococo Room, with admission set at forty cents a head, augmented their earnings and encouraged skiers to stay overnight. The weekend take soon reached the dizzy heights of sixty dollars, with visitors encouraged by Pollough Pogue's lengthy promotional article in the January 24 *Daily Province*. Three hundred on a Sunday was typical by mid-February. Already, Pogue says, they had leased a tract of land on First Lake from West Vancouver for the site of a "mountain inn."

Outside "The Restaurant" at the ski camp in the former Nasmyth Mill, May 1925. (EILIF HAXTHOW COLLECTION)

That spring, bunks installed in one of the cabins provided sleeping room for twenty men, with twelve to fifteen women accommodated in the kitchen. One Friday 1,000 enthusiasts visited Hollyburn. No one ever became rich from skiing at Hollyburn, but the lifestyle was priceless.

While visits dropped off during the summer, the longer days and warmer weather were a welcome change from the winter snow for the ski camp boys. In May 1925, Haxthow writes: "It is hard to imagine any better place as far as day-to-day life goes. The weather is clear and warm, the sun is up by five in the morning. When I poke my nose out of the sleeping bag at seven it is full daylight—no need to linger any longer. When one comes out on the veranda, stretches oneself and breathes in the fresh morning air, then one feels like a million!"

That summer, wanderlust and the need for an income took Haxthow to Saskatchewan where he worked again on the harvest, returning to the ski camp in the fall. Later that fall William Beck, whom Haxthow had met and hired in Saskatchewan, joined the ski camp. Pollough Pogue's enthusiastic article in the *Province* on October 4, 1925, praised the wonders of Hollyburn, causing many people to anticipate good skiing in a snowy winter. But 1925–26 saw El Niño flexing its muscles; Victoria had a run of 652 frost-free days, a record which still stands. It was late January before any skis were rented.

Even before the poor snowfall of 1925–26, Verne displayed his nose for the benefits of networking by arranging in October 1925 for a group of 170, including the West Vancouver City Council and journalists, to visit the ski camp. The reeve made a speech, and the table was decked out with new settings bought for the occasion. Suitably impressed, councillor (later reeve) James B. Leyland donated a cup to be awarded annually to the combined champion in A-class. Later, in 1936, he officially opened the BC championships on Hollyburn. Verne continued to promote the area, and on September 3, 1927, wrote to Leyland describing his plans to arrange an attractive display in the Hudson's Bay Company windows, and a weekly display advertisement in the *Province*. He mentioned the possibility of Prince William of Sweden visiting the camp on horseback. The Prince appears to have had other plans, although the New Zealand All Blacks rugby team did visit in about 1925. In 1929 Verne pushed for park status, nearly a half-century before it actually happened.

Verne's hardworking lieutenant Haxthow was fifty dollars to the good at the end of the 1925–26 year, but he had needed a trap line to supplement his earnings. The preferred catch was marten, but other animals caught included a raccoon. They ate the raccoon which, Pogue stated, tasted a lot like turkey. Much as Haxthow loved Hollyburn, its financial future at this time was uncertain, and in any case he was not ready to settle down. On May 1, 1926, he sold his interests to Verne and left The Restaurant for itinerant labour jobs up the coast.

▲ Skiers on Hollyburn, May 1926.
Rudolph Verne is in the front row,
third from the right. (GEORGE
ARMSTRONG-HILLS COLLECTION)

◀ Margaret and Eilif Haxthow with
their daughter Grace at the cabin
they shared with Ommund and
Margaret Ommundsen, 1935.
(EILIF HAXTHOW COLLECTION)

That fall he built a cabin on Hollyburn, having found a job in August 1926 in the office of the architectural firm of Christensen Ltd. as architect and general contractor. He and Eric Ahlberg had ambitions to build a two-storey hotel on Hollyburn. Although H.C. Christensen drew up preliminary sketches and a first floor plan, the project proceeded no further. Haxthow left Christensen in June 1927 for a brief stint with Boyles Bros. Diamond Drilling. With Ahlberg and two other friends, he also operated for a few months in 1927 the first ski factory in Vancouver. Poor sales ended that enterprise.

Hollyburn imprinted its magic on Haxthow's life, even though his years here were comparatively few. He met Helen Mae Taylor on the mountain; they married in 1934 and had a daughter, Grace, the next year. Resumption of work with Boyles Bros. Diamond Drilling took him away from the West Coast to Ontario in 1938, where he eventually became manager of their Eastern Division. After early retirement in 1951, the family moved back to BC to settle near Duncan. He was a consultant on the plans to blast the navigational hazard Ripple Rock from its place obstructing the shipping lanes near Campbell River, but spent most of his retirement painting, carving and fishing—activities which he had enjoyed on Hollyburn.

Rudolph Verne continued pushing for a better location for the ski camp's headquarters. The Municipality of West Vancouver leased him land at First Lake, a small artificial lake that had been dammed to create a reservoir for Nasmyth's logging flume operations. Verne's Swedish woodsmen compatriots—Oscar Pearson, Ole Anderson and Andrew Irving from the province of Dalarna—dismantled the cookhouse at the mill lower down and moved it in the spring of 1926 up the mountain to the 950-metre level at First Lake. Here not only was the snow better, but they were much closer to the open skiing terrain around First Lake.

A team of horses skidded the timbers up the ridge on a stoneboat, although the sea of mud created by the rains made it hard slogging for the horses. Bricks for the chimney were carried eight at a time. Harold Enquist and Axel Sneis helped build the seventy-five by twenty-five foot (23 metre by 7.6 metre) two-storey camp, and the official opening was held January 16, 1927. A shipment of skis had just arrived, and many visitors strapped on skis the next day for the first time. Snow was good that year—the First Lake snow post still showed fifteen feet in early May. Although the camp was intended as temporary until a permanent log building could be built, the Hollyburn Lodge, substantially unchanged, still survives eighty years later.

Initially christened the Hollyburn Ski Camp, this was the first such camp on the coast in the Pacific Northwest. Besides being the headquarters for the ski club estab-

Hollyburn Ski Camp, ca. 1930.
(VANCOUVER PUBLIC LIBRARY 12724)

lished at this time, it combined a restaurant, a dormitory and a dance hall complete with a gramophone. Above the door the following welcome, created (originally in Swedish) by Oscar Pearson, painted and put up about 1930 by Ray Fraser, epitomized the Scandinavian social philosophy and spirit that imbued Hollyburn:

Be of good cheer   If sad and alone   Here you will find
You're quite welcome here   Let this be your home   A welcome most kind

Norwegian Kaare Hegseth expressed a similar sentiment: "Mining is our bread, and skiing our soul." The original sign lasted until about 1984, and a reproduction was installed in 2000.

Inside the lodge, a mug of eggshell-flavoured Swedish coffee cost ten cents. Pogue writes: "Taken internally, this is a powerful stimulant. After two cups of Oscar's coffee you forget your weariness and are eager for further exertion. Used as a lotion and rubbed on tired limbs it will take away the muscles' soreness and stiffness." Well, maybe. Some skookum root beer made from the local lake water was also available for a nickel a bottle. Bob Tapp recalls this as "slightly thicker than the mud that was in the lake, and tasted about the same."

In the 1920s and 1930s skis rented for twenty-five cents an hour or a dollar for the whole day. Many people needed to rent their equipment since they could not afford to buy their own. Accommodation was basic: twenty-five or fifty cents (accounts vary) bought a night on a mattress of balsam and hemlock boughs spread on planks in the ski camp. Even at that time this was a price that most could afford.

Everything had to be carried in. Packers received one to three cents (later five cents) a pound for their efforts. Average loads were eighty-five pounds, with the legendary record set by George Fanning, who once packed a phenomenal 198 pounds. Skiers had to bring their own blankets, or borrow a horse blanket. Forty males and twelve females could be accommodated overnight. "We slept like sardines, ten in a row, in two tiers." When West Lake Lodge opened in 1933 with real mattresses to sleep on, ski storage (ten cents for the week) generally took over the sleeping space. Few stayed overnight in the lodge after the early '30s.

The skiers ate their lunches in the main ground floor room while a manufactured tin fireplace provided heat and dried mitts. Heat was sporadic, as the kitchen stove

Skiers on Hollyburn, ca. 1928. Brownie Morris, fourth from left, Jack Turner at far right.
(BUDDY BARKER/WIN OLIVER COLLECTION)

Saturday night celebrations at the Hollyburn Ski Camp, early 1940s.
(JOAN GREAVES COLLECTION)

Rudolph Verne, Andrew Irving, Oscar Pearson, Ole Anderson and Axel Sneis in front of the
Hollyburn Ski Camp, 1927. (WEST VANCOUVER ARCHIVES. HOLLYBURN RIDGE COLLECTION. 079.WVA.HRC)

Hollyburn Ski Camp from the top of the First Lake ski jump, ca. 1930.
Several small rental cabins are visible behind the ski camp.
(WEST VANCOUVER ARCHIVES. HOLLYBURN RIDGE COLLECTION. 067.WVA.HRC)

and tin fireplace struggled to burn wet, freshly cut wood, and nights could be uncomfortably cold, but roughing it was part of the experience. The Swedish woodsmen built eighteen small rental cabins from logs near the site to supplement the accommodation. Only one small cabin still remains, and it has been reconstructed. A diving tower at First Lake, also built by the Swedes, and later rebuilt by Fred Burfield, allowed jumpers to take to the air in the summer when the snow had retreated. Many felt that diving was the best summer conditioning exercise for the ski jumper.

The Saturday night stomp, with Scandinavian dances combining with North American steps—square dances, schottisches, polkas, hambos (similar to polkas), waltzes, and jitterbugs—shook the floors until about one a.m., the space packed with lively youth burning off the remainder of their energy. Dancing was mostly to phonograph records on a wind-up gramophone which was powered by batteries packed up to run a six-volt sound system, although on rare occasions an accordion or a small band played. Ski jumper Jack Pratt's wife Peggy, who started going up the mountain in 1940, recalls that dancing at this time was generally to disc jockey Roy Raymer and his records.

Women, enjoying the greater personal freedoms of the 1920s and 1930s, played a full part in Hollyburn life. "Bareheaded, booted and breeched," nearly all had by now, at least for skiing and hiking, shed the encumbering skirts of an earlier generation. Pogue observes in February 1926: "We also argued that the women hikers were better walkers than the men. This was incomprehensible to us, because a majority of them were using ordinary street shoes, many with high heels. . . . Yet they stepped more lightly and seemed to walk with less effort than the men, most of whom trudged heavily along through the mud." Many groups of young women rented cabins, although men always outnumbered women. Margaret Ommundsen recalls that in the winter of 1931–32 cabin rent for four girls was about twenty dollars each for the winter.

Hollyburn during this period had an advantage over Grouse, which entailed a steep and rugged hike (although for a time a road provided car access for the more affluent), and also over Seymour, which required an even longer trek. Access to Hollyburn was relatively benign via the skid road built by the Nasmyth Logging Company from the top of 22nd Street. Many paused for refreshment on their way up at the Forks store, built and operated by Jim Sambrook and his daughter.

When Rudolph Verne could not pay his employees in 1931, Oscar, Ole and Andrew took over the ski camp. Sociable Oscar Pearson, known throughout his life as being a light-footed dancer, provided its public face, while Irving and Anderson generally worked behind the scenes. In the early 1930s Irving returned to Sweden to marry his sweetheart Christina (Stina), then brought her back with him to his Hollyburn cabin. But their options at the ski camp were limited. The District of West Vancouver owned the land on which the lodge was built, and changes could not be made without the District's approval. Although the Swedes paid the District a $500 a year lease, a 1944 request for permission to build a $10,000 extension was put on hold.

Joseph "Pop" Burfield, who had been a locomotive engineer with the CPR in Revelstoke, purchased the Hollyburn Ski Camp and cabins from the three Swedes in 1946. He renamed it Hollyburn Ski Lodge. Anderson, Irving and Stina returned permanently to Sweden. Oscar Pearson also returned to Sweden in 1946, but was attracted back in 1950 to run the new chairlift for Hollyburn Aerial Tramways. He returned to Sweden permanently in 1962 to live out his retirement.

Fred Burfield, a son of the camp's new owners, had moved to West Vancouver from the skiing mecca of Revelstoke; he visited Hollyburn with his family frequently from 1937 on. In 1939 Gus Johnson built him a cabin across First Lake from the Ranger Station, where Fred lived for seven years. He was a ski instructor, and in 1940–41 became one of the first volunteer members and later a part-time supervisor of the first

The Burfield family inside the Hollyburn Ski Lodge, ca. 1946.
L to R: Harry Burfield, "Mom" and "Pop" Burfield, Fred Burfield and Evy Burfield.
(HUGH AIKENS COLLECTION)

aid ski patrol. He also helped ranger Ted Russell with the packing business, using the horses Baldy and Prince, and was himself a ranger for three years.

In 1949 Fred bought a model MC John Deere tractor from Purves Richie for the heavy work at the lodge, which became the main vehicle for bringing supplies up the mountain, invaluable in the construction and maintenance of over twenty log cabins and other buildings. When the tractor was taken out of service it was stored in Cypress's operations yard. Plans are now well underway for its restoration and eventual display near the lodge. A Bombardier half-track was also used for transporting people up the fire access road in winter, and occasionally for providing transportation up the mountain to access skiing on the higher slopes. This Bombardier was sold in 1982 for $100. After extensive reconditioning it continues to provide reliable transportation in Manning Park for its owners.

Many savour memories of the Burfields' blueberry pies and muffins, cooked using berries picked on the hill, and their warming hot apple cider and chili in the winter. By the late 1940s as many as 5,000 hikers and skiers were visiting Hollyburn on a weekend. One busy weekend Fred Burfield did a count, and found that twice as many

Norm Deacon's John Deere, skidding in firewood for Westlake lodge.

visited the Hollyburn area as Seymour and Grouse combined. A New Year's Eve party at the lodge attracted about a hundred people, mostly cabin owners. Skiers often welcomed the New Year by doing midnight ski jumps on the First Lake jump under lighting provided by gas lamps brought out from the dance floor. Brian Creer recalls one year the Norwegians belting out a rousing rendition in Norwegian of "Hail, hail, the gang's all here" from the top of the jump.

The two Burfield sons, Fred and Harry, took over the ski operations on their father Joseph's death in 1954. Harry was an especially accomplished skier who won the local VISKI club race three times. He moved his ski shop to the top of the chairlift when it opened in 1951, but after the chairlift burned down in 1965, he gave up his share and moved to Kamloops, where he operated a ski and sport shop. He lost his life in a plane crash at Tod Mountain (now Sun Peaks) ski area.

"Tall and laconic," Fred Burfield married Evelyn "Evy" Davies on November 12, 1942, and for many years this family was the heart of Hollyburn. Business, however, remained marginal. The lodge's survival was threatened by the decrease in visitors after the demise of the chairlift in 1965, so Fred joined with Gordy Levett and Thorne Schindler to request a grant of $2,500 from the municipality to widen and gravel the road to Hollyburn Ridge so that he could run buses all winter to bring up skiers. With only $1,500 awarded, and heavy snow the next year, the operation proved impractical and closed after one year.

As the lodge aged, the need for major restoration became increasingly clear, but since the land was leased from the District of West Vancouver, Fred Burfield did not have the equity to obtain bank financing for renovations or a new building. Ten-cent coffees and dollar-a-day rentals were hardly enough to impress the banks. In the 1970s he considered applying for a government grant to restore the lodge, but the massive paperwork and bureaucratic hoops deterred him. The years from 1965 to 1973 were quiet ones on Hollyburn, and many municipal officials felt the lodge's days were done. In August 1975 Ken MacLean of West Vancouver's Parks and Recreation Department recommended that Hollyburn Lodge be sold to the provincial government, and demolished if the government did not want it.

Fred stuck it out, and continued to live at and operate Hollyburn Lodge with his vivacious wife Evy, who died of cancer in 1969, and daughter Peggy. He recalls the lodge as a mountain of work: shovelling snow, keeping the trails open, splitting wood for the rented cabins, and running the lodge. Fred brought his daughter up to Hollyburn when she was six weeks old and had her on skis a year later. Peggy, who was born in 1956 and started work at the lodge "as soon as she could see over the counter," recalls her childhood as full of work, but also enriched with many experiences which have become treasured memories.

In 1974 the NDP were elected provincially, bringing a greater sense of government involvement in BC enterprises. Bob Williams, Minister of the Department of Environment, Lands and Parks, decreed that a downhill facility would be created in Cypress Bowl, and Hollyburn remain the cross-country area. Fred continued to operate the lodge, and converted his ski rental to cross-country and hired Nordic instructors. Occasional revivals of the past spirit occurred, such as the BC Mountaineering Club's visit on February 28, 1981, for their annual turkey dinner and ski races:

> There was barely time to open a bottle of cheer before the chow line formed and then it was "devil take the hindmost." As the last morsels were being chewed over the dancing began. . . . The dancing formation formed into a Conga line and this wound around the room until someone opened the door. . . . During these revels the Editor was seen, clad in his own BCMC t-shirt, lying under a table with a Blue Nun.

When Cypress Bowl Recreations Limited purchased the lodge and cross-country ski operation along with the downhill area in 1984, Fred Burfield retired reluctantly to Errington on Vancouver Island. The lodge continues to be open in the winters for day use by cross-country skiers and snowshoers.

❧

Wayne Booth, who took over the operations of Cypress in 1984, saw no future for the lodge. He states that while they tried to make what improvements were possible, the lodge remained far below the existing building codes, with the absence of a proper foundation contributing to its gradual deterioration. He felt that it was not well located, as food and rental services belonged adjacent to the parking lot. In 1995 the province filed a suit alleging that Cypress Bowl Recreations failed to respond to concerns about the structural integrity of the cabins and the lodge. A Planning Commission report that year described the building as too far gone for renovation, recommending CBRL tear it down and produce a replica. When Boyne Resorts took over in 2001, they were no more eager to put money into the lodge.

Fortunately the lodge was not torn down. It endures today, substantially as it was, a mute reminder of its days as the heart of Hollyburn, with the new generations of skiers who glide past or stop for an invigorating cup of hot chocolate and a bite of lunch mostly oblivious to its storied past. Photographs and artifacts adorn the walls, creating a museum atmosphere. On Saturday nights during ski season lively old-time entertainment attracts an appreciative crowd. Hollyburn continues to attract the second largest number of visits of any cross-country area in North America (after Royal Gorge in California), but the lodge has steadily deteriorated.

But wait! Enter the Hollyburn Heritage Society (HHS), riding high on their cross-country skis. Hollyburn veterans Gordon and Iola Knight decided the lodge would not go without a fight. Initially they felt that the building would have to be taken apart and rebuilt in the same style, reusing whatever materials possible. When Iola Knight learned that funding might be available from senior levels of government for heritage restoration, keeping the lodge became a possibility. In 1997 they united with Bob and Greta Tapp to pursue this goal.

They began their awareness efforts at the 1997 Pioneers' Ski Reunion on Mount Seymour, where they sold Hollyburn commemorative coffee mugs and other items to raise funds and to bring to public attention the plight of the lodge. At this time they also began to collect historic photographs of Hollyburn. In 1998 they developed a plan to make the public aware of Hollyburn's history and heritage, and the value of its preservation. West Vancouver Parks and Community Services, through its director Kevin Pike, funded $2,300 of these initial expenses. Bob and Greta Tapp with Gordon and Iola Knight formed the Hollyburn Heritage Society, incorporated under the BC Societies Act in April, 2000, with the mandate to collect the history and artifacts of skiing and other mountain activities on Hollyburn Mountain, and to promote the restoration and preservation of Hollyburn Ski Lodge.

In spite of his previously expressed reservations about the future of the lodge, Wayne Booth of Cypress Bowl Recreations proved receptive to their efforts and, with his support, the Society was awarded $2,567 as part of the Canada Millennium Partnership Program to create a video on the history and heritage of Hollyburn. This was filmed by Bob Cooper of Inglewood Productions and titled "Hollyburn: A Place of Memories." The British Columbia Heritage Trust provided further funding to use some of this footage along with vintage photographs, interviews with old time skiers and narration to produce a video. In recent years Don Grant has actively collected

The dedication of the Hollyburn entrepreneurs' picnic table by Bob Tapp,
far left, August 16, 2003. Gordon Knight is in the centre foreground.
(ALEX SWANSON COLLECTION)

Hollyburn materials and worked tirelessly to promote the cause of Hollyburn. He
has scanned over five thousand photographs of Hollyburn, which have been donated
to West Vancouver Archives. A Helly Hansen Mountain Adventure Award from the
Alpine Club of Canada is assisting Don Grant and others in recording the mountain
experiences of old timers. The Hollyburn Heritage Society also provided the initial
impetus and much of the resource materials for the current book.

Other heritage activities are gathering force as our society is coming to a greater
recognition of the value of preserving the past. In the summer of 2003, grants from the
North Shore Community Foundation and the West Vancouver Rotary Club funded
the installation of a picnic table at First Lake dedicated to early commercial entrepreneurs. The next year the West Vancouver Community Foundation funded the installation of vintage photographs and captions on the yellow cedar banister of the Nasmyth
Bridge which crosses Marr Creek as it leaves First Lake.

The convergence of the Hollyburn Heritage Society's passionate concern and the
2010 Olympics, with snowboarding and freestyle skiing being held next door in the

Cypress downhill ski area, may prove the lodge's salvation. In September 2006 Don Luxton's architectural firm was awarded a contract to make recommendations as to its future. His findings suggest that with the use of new restoration techniques the lodge can indeed be saved, although the price tag of $1,000,000 plus would be at least the cost of a new building. It remains a matter of heated debate as to whether it is better to rebuild a similar structure, or to renovate the existing building.

BC Parks remains unwilling to invest money in a building it does not own, but has awarded $100,000 in 2010 legacy funds, subject to the rest of the funds being raised. The new management of Cypress Bowl Recreations has also become supportive of the plans to retain the building, as has the District of West Vancouver. West Vancouver is currently in negotiations with Cypress to buy the lodge which would then be leased back to Cypress for the ski season. A funding program to restore the building would then be put in place. The future of the lodge looks hopeful.

CHAPTER 4

Outdoor and Ski Clubs

Freedom comes in many forms
When you venture up the hills,
No thoughts of debts or taxes,
Or those ever annoying bills.

—ART "SNEFTY" SENFT'S "THOUGHTS
OF AN OLD TIME SKIER"

Sam Wormington writes in *The Ski Race* that the first skiing in Canada was done by Norwegian Olaf Gjerdrum in 1872 when he worked as an engineer on a railroad construction site. A woodcut of Norwegian A. Birch on skis in Quebec is shown on the cover of *The Canadian Illustrated News* for February 8, 1879—although the name "A. Birch" sounds suspiciously like a fabrication. Hardly Norwegian. BC's earliest skiing took place in the southeast, near the mining towns of Rossland, Kimberley and Revelstoke, where the snow was deep and work in the mines attracted many Scandinavians. Ole Sandberg skied in 1887 from his mineral claims down to Albert Canyon, twenty-one miles east of Revelstoke. At this time the Scandinavians' proficiency in skiing provided transportation to and from mine sites, as well as recreation on their time off.

In 1891 skiers won a race with snowshoers in Revelstoke, encouraging skiers to start a club that year. The Revelstoke Ski Club was not officially incorporated until December 12, 1914, with the Phoenix Ski Club (near Greenwood) founded in 1907, generally recognized as the first in BC. It later folded and moved to Princeton to be reborn as the Amber Ski Club under "Pop" Irwin, although the Phoenix ski hill still operates between Grand Forks and Greenwood. Other early skiing took place in Rossland, with Norwegian miners leading the way. Legendary Olaus Jeldness originated BC's first downhill ski race in 1896 from the top of Red Mountain to Rossland, known as The Jeldness Tea Party (see Appendix 1). A number of ski clubs were organized in BC's interior, but on the West Coast, perhaps because of the mild winters and other recreational opportunities, development was slower.

Clubs were crucial to the development of skiing, as they provided the energy and focus for the development of infrastructure. Club members built accommodations, cut trails, constructed ski jumps, provided instruction and gave an organizing social focus. Between 1900 and 1909, the population of Vancouver tripled, and numerous clubs for sports and other activities developed as a good way for new arrivals to integrate themselves into the community.

The first Vancouver club with an outdoor focus was the Vancouver Mountaineering Club. Its name changed to the British Columbia Mountaineering Club (BCMC) as its focus expanded. Founded in 1907 and incorporated in 1912, the club arranged climbing programs and coordinated the knowledge of trails and routes. In January 1910 they obtained land on Grouse Mountain where that spring they built a cabin. In 1911 Dr. John Davidson, the provincial botanist, formed a botanical section, making the collection of specimens a significant part of many of the outings. This section provided a basis for the Vancouver Natural History Society, which formed an independent association in 1918. Weekend trips were inexpensive and informal, organized to accommodate the majority who worked on Saturday mornings. Members represented a variety of professions, including lawyers, land surveyors, bankers, stenographers, and real estate men, "all gentlemen and gentlewomen." An earnest lot, members also formed geological, entomological, zoological, mapping and meteorological sections.

Frequent weekend trips, in winter generally on snowshoes, were held on the nearby North Shore mountains, especially on Mount Strachan immediately north of Hollyburn. The June 1927 newsletter notes a subcommittee formed to urge the dedication of Hollyburn Ridge as a public park. One of the trails they cut was up Black Mountain from Horseshoe Bay. Trips to Black Mountain, as well as to Mount Strachan via Hollyburn Ridge, took place most years. In 1925, shortly after the Hollyburn Ski Camp opened, fifteen members stayed overnight on the way to the top of Strachan. The newsletter recounts a trip up Hollyburn Mountain on October 12, 1930:

> Fine weather with hours of good visibility added to the enjoyment of those participating in the initial trip of the Winter Schedule to Hollyburn Peak. Lunch at the ski-camp was washed down by a copious supply of hot coffee that has earned Hollyburn an enviable reputation among Vancouver's climbing fraternity. The trail winds pleasantly past little lakelets and sub-alpine meadows to the peak. The crystal clarity of

British Columbia Mountaineering Club cabin on Grouse Mountain, ca. 1920.
(GEORGE BARKER COLLECTION)

the atmosphere revealed all the local peaks brilliantly garbed in their autumnal hues, while the loftier summits were already clothed in winter's mantle of white. The return down Brothers' Creek disclosed new charms and added much to the pleasures of the trip, abundantly rewarding the faithful few for venturing forth.

Other trips took a route from the top of the British Pacific Properties via West Lake to Brothers Creek and Fourth Lake.

On November 16, 1931, the BCMC formed a twenty-member ski section, with Swiss skier Dick Shaich as the instructor—although the BCMC has always been more interested in ski mountaineering than skiing as a separate sport. The ski section made its first trip on December 5, 1931, and appears to have gone on an outing most Sundays. By this time, other clubs—devoted entirely to skiing—had already been formed. There was surprisingly little crossover in membership, although Hollyburn member Jim Pearcy did invite BCMC members to overnight at his cabin on their way up Mount

Strachan on February 11, 1934. Most of the BCMC members appear to have been Anglo-Saxon, as mountaineering was originally a British activity. The ski clubs appealed to the Scandinavian community (but many non-Scandinavians also joined), and attracted those who were more interested in competition, while BCMC members focused on exploring the wilderness and mountain climbing. Generally the latter preferred Mount Seymour.

Another active club, the forerunner of the University of British Columbia's Varsity Outdoor Club, known simply as "The Mountaineering Club," was formed in January 1917, and built their first cabin on Grouse in 1920. After this cabin burned down in 1922, they moved into a cabin by First Lake. After two years they moved back to a cabin higher up on Grouse Mountain, but in the meantime they had, with the BC Mountaineering Club, extended and improved trails to Hollyburn Mountain, Black Mountain, Mount Strachan and the Lions. Many members made annual forays back to Hollyburn.

These early clubs did much more than simply facilitating access to the magnificent terrain of local mountain areas. Vancouver was a booming frontier community attracting a variety of people who were looking for new challenges and new experiences. For the young (or not-so-young) member, the clubs were often outdoor universities. Their members' lives were enriched by association with a diverse cross-section of people from many other cultures and classes in a democratic context which would be less likely to happen back in Europe.

By the mid-1920s the efforts of Rudolph Verne and others were beginning to shape a ski club on Hollyburn. In a 1925 article in the *Province*, Pollough Pogue talks of there being over one hundred members of the Hollyburn Ski Club, which another article refers to as the Hollyburn Snow Birds, but this appears to have been an informal association of like-minded people—not a formalized club. On March 2, 1927, Verne initiated a meeting to form the Hollyburn Pacific Ski Club. White on red were picked as club colours, later changed to white on maroon. Membership fees were set at a very reasonable dollar a year, plus an initiation fee of another dollar. On March 26 of the same year, in a meeting held at Verne's office at 615 West Hastings in Vancouver, the club was officially constituted with fifty members. President H.P. Douglas of the Canadian Amateur Ski Association (CASA) telegrammed from Montreal on April 15, officially recognizing Hollyburn Pacific as the first organized ski club with a mountain headquarters on the Pacific Coast of North America. Rudolph Verne, the new President of the Hollyburn Pacific Ski Club, was appointed a vice-president of the Canadian Amateur Ski Association. West Vancouver reeve V.V. Vinson was made honorary president of the new club, and Ralph Morris was appointed the first club captain.

Perhaps reflecting Verne's Swedish background, the club promoted a strong presence in cross-country skiing as well as ski jumping. As stated in the club's rules and regulations: "In the Club's opinion, Cross Country skiing should receive first consideration, and should at least be on even terms with jumping. The club in its desire to bring cross country skiing back to its proper place is particularly fortunate in having within its radius the finest territory for Cross Country skiing in the Dominion." While still in its fledgling stages at Hollyburn, ski jumping, especially for those with Norwegian backgrounds, was also an integral part of the skiing experience.

Verne was a great Hollyburn enthusiast. He reported in 1929 that the West Vancouver Council had gone on record as supporting the "reservation of the plateau as a national park." He argued in the 1928 *Canadian Amateur Ski Association* journal that Hollyburn had everything that St. Moritz, Switzerland (the site of the 1928 Winter Olympics), had. He envisioned the possibility of "easy accessibility by means of overhead incline automatic railways which in twenty minutes could bring thousands of [Vancouver's] residents and visitors up to the wonderful scenic and sportive resources on the mountain plateau." He might have been pleased to know that by 2010 many of his dreams will have been realized.

A feisty supporter of western interests, Verne helped put western Canadian skiing on the national radar. Although western Canadian skiers often dominated in competition, the administration and the bulk of the skiers remained in eastern Canada. Verne, along with presidents of other ski clubs, was asked to nominate a skier from the west for the four-man team to represent Canada in skiing at the 1928 Winter Olympics in St. Moritz. Verne suppressed his bias towards cross-country skiing enough to select Olav Tellefsen, a jumper recently arrived from Norway and a member of the Hollyburn Pacific Ski Club that was rapidly making its presence felt on both the local and the national scene. When Tellefsen was not one of the four (all Eastern) skiers selected to Canada's Olympic team, Verne mounted an active lobby on his behalf. A flurry of telegrams between Verne and CASA did not produce the results he desired and, reportedly because of "passport trouble," Tellefsen never did travel to the Olympics.

Verne's failure to place Tellefsen on the Olympic squad apparently convinced him that Western interests would not be protected within the structure of the Canadian Amateur Ski Association as it was. His efforts to change this led to the formation of the western branch of CASA October 19, 1928, in a meeting at the original Vancouver Hotel, with representatives from Revelstoke, Jasper, Banff, Burns Lake, Camrose and Vancouver.

In January 1933, Verne and his rebellious westerners took the further step of form-

ing a completely independent Western Canadian Amateur Ski Association (WCASA).
Verne was elected president. Verne's proposal that they bid farewell to the Canadian
Ski Association and join the Amateur Athletic Union of Canada (AAUC) apparently
went too far for his colleagues, and was turned down by the WCASA. He resigned and
set up an outlaw association, but the only club to join was the Viking Club, which was
an offshoot of the athletic club that Verne belonged to himself. The Western Canadian Amateur Ski Association disbanded April 22, 1935, and Verne withdrew from
skiing politics. The Vancouver Ski Club newsletter *The Bushwacker* notes his visiting
Hollyburn in 1939, the first time in six years. He returned to his native Stockholm in
the spring of 1947.

Most of those who discovered skiing in these years were no doubt blissfully oblivious
to the political battles waged by Verne and others. By 1934 two main runs provided
opportunities for accessible skiing. The shorter Grand National traversed the mountain from the Hollyburn Ski Camp at First Lake to the new ski lodge at West Lake.
The longer one, which climbed two-and-half miles (four kilometres) from the Holly-

Hollyburners at the Northwest Championships on Grouse Mountain,
April 14, 1933. L to R: Druce Cooke, Bill Hansen, Nordal Kaldahl, Rudolph Verne.
The others are unidentified. (DRUCE COOKE COLLECTION)

burn Ski Camp at First Lake north to the summit of Hollyburn, was further developed as a one-chain-wide (sixty-six feet, or twenty metre) swath by the Young Men's Forestry Branch in 1937. The present Wells Gray run, as it was later named for the minister of lands, follows this route from the junction of Grand National and Sitzmark to the Powerline, then above the Powerline to the junction of Triangle and Pacific. Above this point to the out-of-bounds area the trail is named Romstad's.

Equipment was basic and relatively cheap; the reasonable price of twenty-five dollars for top racing skis compensated for the frequency of broken skis before laminates became common. Jim Harman recalls breaking two pairs of rental skis in one day. Some skiers made their own from flat pieces of maple or ash-sawn lumber, the wood often purchased from Fyfe Smith's hardwood company. The planks were clamped at both ends and soaked in a bathtub; a soup can or two-by-four in the middle of the two skis maintained the camber. Jumping skis were longer and heavier, while downhill and cross-country used the same skis. A few skied on curved barrel staves.

Ski wax was often paraffin wax over a pine tar base—even Johnson's floor wax was used. Footwear was generally logging or hiking boots strapped directly onto the skis—Buddy Barker recalls that she tied her skis on with rope. Not surprisingly, the unstable support led to many fractured ankles.

Common garb until about 1933 was riding breeches with army-style leg-covering tapes called puttees, calf-high boots and Huitfeldt bindings. Jackets and sweaters were of the everyday variety except for club sweaters. The BCMC newsletter noted that "it has been the general opinion among Mountaineering Club members for some years that the rougher and tougher you looked the more efficient you were in the hills. Male and female alike turned out in ghastly assortments of patched and baggy pants, ripe old jackets and antique, battered hats."

While only the top skiers competed in the big meets, many took part in the local club competitions and, of course, everybody partied. Outings were organized every Sunday to acquaint skiers with the area, and First Lake was a popular place to skate if cold weather preceded the snow. During the week, clubs organized dances, swimming parties, hockey games, bowling outings, an inter-club softball league, work parties, an annual picnic at Belcarra Park and an annual banquet—not much down time for those who loved activity! The Commodore on Granville Street in Vancouver was a popular place for dances, with over 500 skiers attending the kick-off dance for the 1934–35 season. Love's Café at 823 Granville was a popular rendezvous for Thursday lunches. This was "family and friendship" skiing.

By the mid-1930s Hollyburn skiers had built many cabins. After a Saturday of vigorous skiing, many headed back to their cabins or the ski camp to have supper and get ready for the dance at the lodge. Although lack of money limited the drinking of most, Harry Collins recalls the dubious joys of skiing back to their cabins after a

Chivalry in the snow on Hollyburn, ca. 1926. A young man tightens a primitive ski binding for one of the ladies. (GEORGE ARMSTRONG-HILLS COLLECTION)

liquor-lubricated evening of dancing. "In moonlight all you could see through the trees were patches of white and patches of black, and you couldn't tell what was in the black areas. It was like Russian roulette. . . . We'd get home bruised and bleeding, but we always made it in one piece. Back at the cabin we'd fire up the stove and sit down to a game of poker till two or three in the morning." Occasional amateur nights were lively displays of various talents. "Those grapefruit gals, the Moron Matrons, Les May and Bud McInnes brought down the house and raised a blush on the cheeks of Ken Arnott, with a strip tease that rates World Fair billing" (*The Bushwacker*, January 18, 1940). The Hollyburn Pacific Ski Club grew rapidly in the initial years, reaching 600 members at its peak.

While the Hollyburn Pacific Club members enjoyed great competitive success in the local ski jumping, cross-country and downhill events, some of the less talented resented the star performers receiving a disproportionate share of the club membership fees

Bud MacInnes (left) and Les May perform before an enthusiastic crowd at the
VISKI club cabin, ca. 1940. (BUD AND NAOMI MACINNES COLLECTION)

and other support for their travel and competition, especially when some of the stars
were itinerants who stayed around for only a year or two. Some even described the
problem as "racial," for most of the star competitors were recent arrivals from Scan-
dinavia. The onset of the Depression and the shrinking resources available may have
accentuated the tension.

A split developed between the executive, who supported the status quo, and much
of the membership, who favoured a more democratic allocation of resources. At a
meeting in 1930 some members made plans to oust the old executive in favour of a
new slate. Al Twist recalls the tension of this meeting in the December 15, 1939, *Bushwacker*:

> At this crowded meeting, the electric atmosphere of which I shall never forget, this
> [the ousting of the old executive] was attempted. A new executive was nominated
> from the floor, including the old Secretary.

Vancouver Ski Club cabins at First Lake, 1940s. The VISKI lodge in the centre is flanked on the left by the women's quarters and on the right by the men's quarters.
(WEST VANCOUVER ARCHIVES. WEST VANCOUVER ARCHIVES COLLECTION. 0358.WVA.PHO)

But the matter was out of our hands. At private gatherings, the clique had decided to break the club wide open, and to form a new organization from the fragments, hoping particularly to eliminate the more outspoken, democratic members of the old body.

The executive offered to resign, proposing that another election be held. When the membership refused the offer, the old executive broke away to form the Vancouver Ski Club, or the VISKIS as its members came to be called.

Most of the top jumpers, including the Norwegian stars (but not Nordal Kaldahl), joined the new Vancouver Ski Club, which became especially known for its jumping. Hollyburn Pacific also continued to post good results, and attracted and held stars like Daisy Johnson (née Bourdon), Harry Burfield and Jack Pratt. Friendly competition in any case soon replaced the initial acrimony.

The Vancouver Ski Club's membership of 217 in 1939 made it the largest club in

Skiers bound for competition at a train station in the early 1940s. L to R back row: Norm Deacon, Bill Chapman, Russ Little, Bus Lind, Bill Irwin. Middle row: Joan Sheffield, Maurita Stricken, Daisy Johnson, Jenny Lind, June Gillrie, Bea MacIntosh. Front row: Paddy Wing, Brownie Cleary, Eric MacInn. (JUNE GILLRIE COLLECTION)

the Vancouver ski zone. Nineteen men carried a piano on poles up to the Vancouver Ski Club's cabin at First Lake, although its musical quality never recovered from its trip. Accommodation for the ski season from November 1 to May 1 remained a reasonable eleven dollars, with a nightly rate of sixty cents rising to seventy-five cents in 1938. Maroon sweaters identified the Hollyburn Pacific Ski Club, while the Vancouver Ski Club sported blue. Both sported white Vs.

The VISKIS routinely entered more competitors in events than any other northwest club. In the 1930s no government or commercial subsidies for travel or equipment defrayed their costs. Neither this nor the rough and rutted roads and uncertainties of train travel stopped them from travelling to wherever there was a tournament—Wells, Revelstoke, Princeton, Rossland, Mount Baker, Mount Rainier, Leavenworth or Spokane. The first ski trains to Banff started in about 1933, with the trips combining skiing with some extreme partying. The total cost for the first Banff trip, including beer, rooms and meals, was $17.35 a person, thanks to accommodation by Brewsters, owners of Banff's Mount Royal Hotel. Many of the trips were arranged by Hollyburn member Gerry Hardman, who was a sales rep for Canadian Pacific Railways.

Membership in the Hollyburn Pacific Ski Club dropped off in the first years of the Depression after the formation of the Vancouver Ski Club. Many, especially those employed in logging and mining, also left in search of employment. But in 1934 a club report in the Canadian Ski Year Book states that membership in the Hollyburn Pacific Ski Club had doubled in the past two years, and was back to its 1930 level— no doubt helped by a fees reduction in 1933 from four dollars back to the original dollar. Bill Dudgeon, president after the Vancouver Ski Club split off, brought business organization to the club that helped to bring in new members.

Newsletters played an important role in fostering a sense of community for both clubs. In 1932 the Vancouver Ski Club initiated *Snowflakes*, the first ski publication on the West Coast. While short-lived, this was soon followed by *Hiker and Skier*, edited by Pollough Pogue. *Hiker and Skier* lasted for ten years, during which time it reported the activities of the entire skiing community of BC and Alberta, provided an important forum for exchanging event results and club news and gave the growing number of western clubs a sense of connection. The number of ski clubs in western Canada grew from seven in 1927–28 to forty-five in 1939.

The Hollyburn Booster Committee initiated *The Bushwacker*, a monthly newsletter for the Hollyburn Pacific Ski Club, in 1938. Complementing the *Hiker and Skier*, which had more information on competition and was aimed at a provincial audience, this newsletter focused on juicy gossip concerning the social and personal lives of members of the Hollyburn Pacific Club. In the newsletter, "bushwacking" was not bushwhacking in the usual sense of hacking one's way through pathless bush. "Bushwacking" was socializing, going from cabin to cabin, an activity which embodied much of the communal good-times spirit of Hollyburn. With an eye to shortages caused by wartime rationing, a writer commented in the December 1942 issue, "let's make bushwacking resolution number one for 1943. We may search a long time before we'll find another place where there's a warm welcome inside EVERY door, so let's make the most of the spirit of Hollyburn, and take our own sugar."

The communal atmosphere was enhanced by a new clubhouse for Hollyburn Pacific Ski Club, completed in 1936 by Gus Johnson, Nordal Kaldahl and Tom Gibson at the top of what later became the Jack Pratt ski hill near First Lake. Ted Russell and his horse Baldy brought up the logs for the building from farther down the mountain, a difficult uphill job. When finished, the main floor included a living room and kitchen, with sleeping accommodations upstairs. The roof doubled as the in-run for the club jumping hill.

In late 1944, because the clubhouse was on the edge of Brothers Creek watershed, the municipality of West Vancouver required that it be moved. In return they were given a new location plus a 9/10 acre lot in the private property area of the mountain. Assisted by a $400 grant from the West Vancouver Municipal Council, the cabin was taken apart by Ted Russell and, with the help of his workhorse, Old Red, moved to its current site on the main trail. Here it was reconstructed by Ottar and Emil Brandvold, and served as club quarters until 1963, when it was leased, then sold in 1965 to the Burnaby girl guides. Still in good condition, it is now known as Burn-a-bee Chalet.

The weekend getaways of young men and women encouraged much socializing. Romance often bloomed among the moguls or elsewhere, and many people found their future mates in the cabins and on the ski slopes. It may have been a little harsh to say (as some did) that there were the good girls, and then there were the girls that went to Hollyburn, but those who weekended up the mountain definitely enjoyed a rich social life. Both men and women recall these days with a nostalgia sweetened by the intervening years.

~

At first, each club organized its own ski events, but as the initial energy flagged, it soon became obvious that co-operation would save a lot of needless effort. There were only so many officials and judges, and only so much organizing energy to spread around. In the winter of 1934 all the ski clubs on the North Shore mountains joined in putting on highly successful skiers' dances, with a repeat the following fall. On February 23, 1938, the two Hollyburn clubs formed the "Ski Promotion Committee of Hollyburn Ridge" to eliminate the unproductive competition between the clubs and the unnecessary work needed to keep two operations going. Jack Hutchinson represented the Vancouver Ski Club, and Fred Hudson Hollyburn; tournaments were conducted jointly.

Membership in both clubs was decimated by World War II, with over one-third of Hollyburn Pacific members joining the Services—many not to return. The lack of fuel curtailed travel to wartime competitions and, in addition, warm-weather winters from 1940–42 limited skiing. Plans to merge the two clubs began in 1940.

Diminishing membership in the Hollyburn Pacific Club in the fall of 1944 hastened its amalgamation with the Vancouver Ski Club in November 1945 to form the Cypress Ski Club; the name reverted to the Vancouver Ski Club in 1948. A membership of 360 at the end of 1946 made it the largest ski club in western Canada. One goal of the amalgamation was to provide a louder voice to convince the provincial government to fund the development of the growing sport of downhill skiing in its present location on Cypress.

A newsletter started in 1945, *The Cypress Log*, was renamed *Ski Trails* in 1948; it was a professional production that provided an excellent forum for club happenings.

At this time there were three major annual club tournaments. The Hollyburn open jumping was held on the First Lake jumping hill, with the club championships on the Ridge. Perhaps the best test of a skier's ability was the VISKI Classic, first run in 1938, from the peak of Hollyburn to Hollyburn Lodge, which attracted many of the top male and female skiers both locally and from away. This combined an initial steep downhill with a challenging two-mile cross-country trek. The race was cancelled in 1955 and 1956 because of waterboard restrictions. It was revived in 1957, but in a shortened form—only the downhill section was run.

Gradually the energy required to mount these events began to flag. Nothing could recapture the magic of the 1930s. The newsletter carried frequent laments about the declining membership and the lack of club spirit. Seymour sold 63 percent of the tickets for the 1949 Skiers' Fall Ball, Grouse 24 percent, and the Vancouver Ski Club clocked in at an embarrassing 13 percent. The November 1951 *Ski Trails* lamented that "unless help is forthcoming in the very near future any work that has to be done will have to be paid for and this means that money which would ordinarily be spent to send competitors to tournaments or to provide prizes, etc., for the club will be cut down."

Annual funfest regattas beginning in August 1949 at First Lake attempted to regenerate the former spirit and camaraderie. Three hundred attended the second regatta on August 20, 1950, with swim teams representing Vancouver swim clubs com-

First Lake Regatta, early 1950s. (FRED AND ETHEL JONES COLLECTION)

ing up to compete. Among the events were diving exhibitions, swimming competitions, jousting and a log rolling contest. In another event, the "baby" race, swimmers dressed in nightgowns and bonnets swam across the lake, drank the formula out of a baby bottle and then swam back to the start. Men competed in outrageous drag for the title of "Lady of the Lake," a spoof based on the poem by Sir Walter Scott. The winner "warmed" the lake with a kettle of boiling water. Another event, the Mardi Gras, held at Westlake Lodge around the beginning of May, heralded the end of ski season; it always featured an exhilarating water fight. Yearly outings to Bowen Island and Belcarra Park provided an opportunity for intermountain softball competitions, and an interclub softball league was active.

But these events did not compensate for the ski club's struggles as the fifties wore on, which were aggravated by the opening of the new chairlift in 1951. The chairlift diminished the need for overnight accommodation. During the same period the *Vancouver Sun* and *Province* newspapers ran successful ski schools on the North Shore mountains, which filled the need for instruction. The only real function left for the club was to provide organization for social events, and here a growing number of other options competed in the post-war world. The 1950–51 club membership of 193 declined to fifty-nine in 1955–56, although it was up slightly to seventy-three in 1957–58. An even greater concern was the lack of new juniors—the future of the club. President Jim Hennigar lamented in the January 1953 newsletter:

> Enthusiasm seems to have vanished from most people on the mountain, and we are content to let other people go out and do our jobs, or things that we should take on ourselves as our jobs.

Relations with other groups were also prickly. The club refused a 1952 request from the Canadian Amateur Ski Association to help fund Olympic expenses because of "inefficient organization with respect both to team selection and financial arrangements displayed by [the administrative office in] Montreal." This contrasts with the unstinting generosity (see below, pp. 87–88) with which club members and others supported Tom Mobraaten's trip to the 1936 Olympics.

Plans to build a world-class jumping trestle at West Lake bogged down, although eventually the mid-level Jack Pratt jump was completed near First Lake in 1958. Most races ended in the 1950s, with the VISKI Classic last run in 1961. The Vancouver Ski Club was dissolved in 1965, its last president Jack Rockandel. On November 4, 1965, the assets of $2,613.50 and the acre-sized lot they had been given with the new lodge location were donated to Simon Fraser University (SFU) for an athletic scholarship. Simon Fraser held off selling the lot, which turned out to be a good decision, as when they finally sold it in 1991 to the District of West Vancouver they realized $19,500. The money was split between a perpetual scholarship fund for members of the SFU ski team and the defrayment of administrative and equipment costs of the ski team.

A number of clubs continue to function today. On the cross-country side, the main club in recent decades has been the Nordic Racers, which combines recreation with friendly competition. It has maintained a fluctuating membership of around two hundred. Current activities include ski improvement sessions, Tuesday night races and Wednesday club nights. The West Coast Nordic Club, which branched off from this club, includes about twenty-five generally younger members who are more interested in serious competition, especially biathlon (cross-country skiing and shooting). The Jack Rabbit Ski Club is part of a national organization that instructs the younger set in cross-country skiing. Currently they have about 500 members, including 290 aged four to fourteen, instructed by more than seventy volunteer coaches. Snowshoeing has also burgeoned in popularity, with perhaps 10 percent of those using the Nordic area finding this their preferred way of exploring the outdoors.

Downhill skiing takes place not at Hollyburn but at nearby Cypress Bowl. The Cypress Ski Club, founded in 1986, works to increase the skill level and competitive success of young skiers. The current president is Colin Boyd and the program director is Shona Crawford. One of the most successful ski clubs in the country, the Cypress Ski Club in 2005 was named Alpine Canada's club of the year, and in 2007 won event of the year. Colin Boyd credits this success to their first-class volunteers and coaches, and Cypress's great terrain. He states that a sense of community continues at Cypress; when he skis there he always meets people he knows.

Currently about four hundred young people and their parents enjoy the various downhill programs, which include the Nancy Greene Program for ages six to twelve, K-1 for ages eleven to twelve and K-2 for ages thirteen to fourteen. There is also a joint North Shore International Ski Federation team for young people aged fifteen to nineteen who are going on to more serious competition. In addition, there is an adult improvement program primarily for parents who want to improve their skills. Some entry-level snowboarding instruction is also given. Six full-time coaches are available for instruction. Activities include dryland training in the summer, mountain biking, a surf camp at Long Beach and a ski trip to France in the fall.

Competitive freestyle skiing and snowboarding began in about 1998. It developed in conjunction with the Olympic bids, with Tanya Callon in charge of the Vancouver Freestyle Club. In 2002, two-time Olympian Ryan Johnson was hired to run an advanced program at Cypress. A First Nations snowboard team also uses this area on occasion, and the Vancouver Adaptive Snow Sports Society offers programs for people with disabilities on Cypress and the other North Shore mountains.

While these clubs certainly perform valuable functions in providing a place for skiers to develop and display their skills, they do not create the all-encompassing way of life in the manner of the Hollyburn and Vancouver ski clubs in the pre-World War

Hollyburn Ridge Association's Loggers' Sports at First Lake, September 1998.
(GERRY HARDMAN COLLECTION)

Pioneer Skiers' Reunion at First Lake, September 20, 1995.
(GERRY HARDMAN COLLECTION)

II days. People come together for their training and recreation and then go about their busy lives.

The spiritual children of the earlier clubs are the mountain bike clubs, especially the North Shore Mountain Bike Association, and other clubs such as the North Shore Riders, which embody much of the camaraderie and anarchic *joie de vivre* of the earlier ski clubs. Like the ski clubs, they are organizations that not only bring together people enthused by a sport but also foster a way of life relying heavily on the initiative of individual members. They operate with minimal government or business support, building and maintaining their own trails. Even the spectacular jumps and other stunts they perform at venues such as West Vancouver's Coho Festival recall the ski jumpers of times past.

❧

In the 1970s the Tapp family organized the Loggers Sports Days, which were adopted by the Hollyburn Ridge Association to keep some of the earlier Hollyburn spirit alive. Sports at this fall festival include tug-of-war, nail driving, cross-cut saw contests and axe throwing. Log rolling was also practised some years. This event is now called the "First Lake Fall Festival." Many of the pioneers turn up annually, often with their children, their grandchildren and even their great-grandchildren. While these festivals may not have the same excitement as those of the early days, they are pleasant occasions to get together, renew old acquaintances and reminisce about the good times of the past. Bob Tapp has been active in Hollyburn organizations from the time he first went up on Good Friday 1942. The Tapp family have owned their current cabin, Holmenkollen, since 1961.

Another event that attempts to recapture the earlier Hollyburn communal enthusiasm is the annual reunion of old-time skiers from Hollyburn, Grouse and Seymour. This event was spearheaded in 1992 by Naomi and Bud McInnes. In 1997 Alex Douglas held this reunion on Mount Seymour, and it has since alternated between Hollyburn and Seymour. These reunions have fostered an excellent means for both groups to publicize their purpose of collecting history and heritage and are often lively events in which old friends exchange reminiscences of the days when they were kings.

CHAPTER 5

West Lake/Westlake:
The Other Lodge

*No, no caviar at Westlake—just good, clean, wholesome fun, fresh
air, exercise, and dreamless, health-giving sleep.*

—1930s BROCHURE

T he growing popularity of skiing and the growing demand for overnight
accommodation fostered by the Hollyburn Ski Camp opened up the possibilities
for another camp. West Lake, at an elevation of 850 metres and an easy fifteen minutes of mostly downhill skiing from Hollyburn Ski Camp, was an accessible and
available location. Ron Brewis approached North Vancouver pioneer and entrepreneur Edward Mahon with plans to build a lodge on the south shore of West Lake—
so named because it was at the west end of 400 acres (162 hectares) of land the latter
owned. Brewis was an all-around athlete and not primarily a skier—he was captain
of his college cricket team, played rugby and water polo, and was involved with the
formation of the Vancouver Amateur Swimming Club, the West Vancouver Tennis
Club and the Denman Tennis Club.

When Mahon proved receptive to the plan, Brewis started by damming West
Lake, enlarging it to two acres. Brewis hired F. Barr and Alan "Bus" Young to build
a trail up from 15th Street to West Lake, but because the trail was rough and long, the
existing 22nd Street trail was preferred for packing materials. He contracted three

Horseback riders visit West Lake Lodge, 1930s.
(JOAN MATHEWS COLLECTION)

Finns, Axel Nordmann, Emil Ronn and "Shorty," and paid them $1.25 a day to build the lodge at West Lake. Construction started in September 1932, and continued over a winter which saw seven metres of snow. All were quartered in the D'Aoust cabin, about a half mile east of Hollyburn Ski Camp, rented for ten dollars a month. With everything having to be packed in, building the lodge at West Lake was a major challenge.

Florence Brewis recalls that it snowed so much that the increasing depth of the snow kept pace with the rising walls of the lodge. To get rid of the snow that filled the inside, Brewis built fires outside the walls to melt the snow, creating large craters into which the snow from inside could be shovelled. The roof was fashioned from red cedar shakes sledded in from a stand below the 450-metre level, and the floors from yellow cedar. The main room was twelve metres by six metres, with two wings five-and-a-half by five-and-a-half metres, one for the kitchen and the other for overnight accommodation.

Opening on the weekend of March 18, 1933, West Lake Lodge had accommodation for sixteen in each of four rooms at a dollar a night. In April, Brewis's purchase of bunk beds and mattresses from a defunct mining company brought new luxury to mountain living. Cedar-bough beds were now relegated to the past, and even blankets were provided. It is likely that with these relatively sumptuous accommodations, not to mention the boom in construction of rental and private cabins, the use of Hollyburn Ski Camp for overnight accommodation soon ended.

Two dozen sets of skis purchased from Flaa and Hagen in Vancouver rented for thirty-five cents for the first hour, and twenty cents for each additional hour. Starting in November 1934, music for the Saturday night dances was provided by the West Lake Harmony Orchestra. A generator supplied power. The main room was later extended to provide more accommodation, as well as a second kitchen where overnighters could cook their own food. In January 1935, when seventy-five new pairs of skis were acquired, a six-metre by nine-metre addition became Fred and Harry Jones' ski rental room, and extended the length of the building to thirty metres. Cabins were also built for rentals.

Jack Summerfield cleared the land for a ski jump on the north side of the lake, and Irish Beaumont and Pollough Pogue's son Mickey built the biggest trestle on Hollyburn. West Vancouver reeve J.B. Leyland officially opened it on January 27, 1934, and on March 11 the Vancouver City championships brought 2,000 spectators up the West Lake trail from the top of 15th Street. Nordal Kaldahl took top honours and the West Lake trophy that Brewis had donated. In October 1934, Olaf Moen's addition to the jump raised the trestle by three metres, making it the largest in the Lower Mainland, with jumps of over fifty metres now possible. West Lake Ski Lodge advertised itself as "The Home of BC's Champion Ski Jumpers." Revelstoke's elite would likely disagree, but for Lower Mainland skiers, at least, it became the jump of choice for training and competition.

On March 16, 1937, Edward Mahon died. Because of ill health he had not been to the lodge for eighteen months. Mrs. Mahon and her son Bryan decided to sell. Brewis himself could not raise the purchase money, but he helped Fred and Harry Jones to buy the lodge. The original West Lake Ski Camp closed permanently May 1, 1938, when the West Vancouver Municipality objected to its presence in their proposed extension of the Brothers Creek watershed. At this time the District of West Vancouver was not connected to the Greater Vancouver Water Board, and obtained its domestic water supply from the Brothers Creek system, of which West Lake is a part. The loss of the West Lake site meant abandoning Hollyburn's marquee jump— a major setback to the development of ski jumping in this area. Florence Brewis states in her article "The Other Side of the Mountain" published in *Pioneer News* October/November 1995:

> In lieu of a cash commission of the sale, Mr. Brewis requested that he have the two
> 80-acre blocks that sloped south and away from Brothers Creek. This was agreed

The new Westlake Lodge, September 6, 1943.
(WEST VANCOUVER ARCHIVES COLLECTION. 0262.WVA.PHO)

upon. His plan was to develop cabins to rent on the property. Then Fred and Harry Jones approached him with the idea of purchasing ten acres on the north border of the block closest to the original West Lake site.

The Jones brothers dismantled the original lodge and sledded the reusable logs on the snow to the new site about 300 metres south, where, reconstructed, it became the ski shop.

Some of the cabins at the old site were also dismantled and reassembled to be used as rentals. The Jones brothers also built a magnificent twenty-one metre by nine metre two-storey lodge, christened the Westlake (one word) Ski Lodge, although it was not actually at West Lake—a cause for confusion to many visitors over the years. Thirty-centimetre logs cut from the site were used in construction, with the 13.5-metre ridgepole weighing 225 kilograms. The twelve-metre-long first section was completed in 1938, and the other nine metres were added the next summer. Only flooring and windows were packed in; everything else was hewn from the site. Its rustic beauty made it for many a treasured part of skiing life on the North Shore for almost a half-century.

A new run, "The Graveyard," was cleared for the growing popularity of down-hill and slalom. While weekends remained the busiest time, many also came up on Wednesdays, when stores were closed for the afternoon, with many accessing the

Routes to West Lake Lodge, 1930s.
(WEST VANCOUVER ARCHIVES COLLECTION. 188.WVA.DOC)

West Lake Lodge postcard, mid 1930s.
(JOAN MATHEWS COLLECTION)

lodge via a trail from the British Properties. Unfortunately its 850-metre elevation, 100 metres lower than Hollyburn, often made for marginal snow conditions.

The Jones brothers sold out in 1949 to Don Lee, who had previously owned the Forks store. Don Lee soon found himself in financial trouble at Westlake, so the bank persuaded Norm Deacon to take over the lodge. He did so on May 1, 1952, and set about improving the cabins and developing ski runs. Deacon, who also worked as an upholsterer, had a long history with Hollyburn, having built a cabin on private property, which, with other neighbourhood cabins, became known as Deaconville. He was a director of the ski patrol for eight years and also built and operated ski tows. Bert Baker recalls him as extremely industrious, building tows, buying a "cat" that kept the trails in decent shape, and generally doing more than anyone else for the Westlake Ski Lodge area.

At this time the lodge could sleep seventy, in rooms that housed four or five each, at a dollar a night. Guests could buy meals at the coffee shop or do their own cooking. A generator provided power. The Westlake Ski Club operated out of the lodge in the 1930s and '40s, and changed its name to Hollyburn Ski Club after the Hollyburn

Pacific Ski Club and Vancouver Ski Club merged. The club folded when the ski lift burned down in 1965, but the lodge remained for over twenty years as the only resort facility on the mountain to provide overnight accommodation.

Ron Caverly, who had been frequenting Hollyburn since 1947, sold his television repair service and purchased the lodge in 1972. He changed its name to Cypress Park Resort after the opening of the new highway in 1973. Clients could now drive up the highway and then take the resort vehicle—making the trip only an hour from downtown Vancouver. Caverly's improvements to the lodge and facilities included a full-course dining room and licensed premises, as well as improved overnight accommodation. But business remained slow. Without assurance from the municipality that he would be able to continue to operate, he was reluctant to sink money into major changes. He sold out in 1985 to the McCann family and moved to Galiano Island, where he operated a motel.

Shortly after the McCanns bought the lodge from Caverly, it burned to the ground on the night of October 20, 1986. The fire probably started by sparks landing on the roof from the chimney. West Vancouver Council decided against granting any rezoning that would allow the lodge to be rebuilt, and so ended the story of Westlake Ski Lodge.

CHAPTER 6

Heroes of the Harnessed Hickory: Competitive Camaraderie

☙

The beginner who runs in a cross country race may find the going hard but finishes a far better skier than when he started. Racing is the best practice.

—*HIKER AND SKIER*, JANUARY 10, 1935

Cross-country skiing and ski jumping mushroomed in western Canada after World War I, with the Norwegians leading the way. In the nineteenth and early twentieth centuries Scandinavians had practised ski jumping as an extension of cross-country, a natural way of clearing obstacles on the cross-country route. Most early jumps were relatively small, but larger trestles soon pushed skiers to longer jumps. Jumping became the premier event of most tournaments at Hollyburn. The often spectacular flights (and falls) of jumpers attracted appreciative crowds. From 1927 to about 1960 the talents of immigrant Norwegians and others made skiing—both jumping and cross-country—immensely popular in the Pacific Northwest.

Tournaments were festive events, often attracting thousands of enthusiastic fans and top-level competitors, both local and visitors, occasionally including athletes from Europe. John Snersnud, Olympic medallist from Finland, made exhibition jumps at Hollyburn in March 1929. Olav Ulland, former world champion and at that time living in Seattle, competed in a Hollyburn meet in 1946. Other Scandinavian stars were exchange students. Ski jumping and races in downhill, cross-country, and later slalom

Men's ski race on Hollyburn, January 1, 1928. L to R Jack Turner (No. 1), Walt Kennedy (No. 4), Bill Cripp (No. 5), Gordon Billingsley (No. 2), Finn Fladmark (No.,11), Harry Collins (No. 8). Buddy Barker is seated in front. The others are unidentified.
(WIN OLIVER/BUDDY BARKER COLLECTION)

provided incentive for both the luminaries and the weekend warriors to get out and enjoy pushing each other to greater accomplishments.

Rudolph Verne organized and promoted the first ski race in Vancouver in Stanley Park in 1924 (apparently a good snow year), perhaps inspired by the first Winter Olympics that were held that year at Chamonix, France. Eight competed before 1,500 spectators.

The first race on Hollyburn took place early in March 1927, from First Lake up to the snow post at Sixth Lake and back, four miles of skiing along unpacked trails. The first sanctioned Canadian Amateur Ski Association (CASA) cross-country race for men in western Canada, with twenty competitors, was held April 17, 1927. Rudolph Verne nostalgically recalls this race in the *Vancouver Sun* of February 8, 1947:

Those fortunate enough to be present will never forget the recurrent gaiety and sheer admiration centred around one Abe Knight, cocky and wise-cracking; or quiet

The starting line-up for the first women's ski race on Hollyburn, April 1928. Daisy Bourdon (No. 6), Kitty Franklin (No. 2), Buddy Barker (No. 4), Millie Kennedy (No. 10). Also in photo: Doris Parkes, Dorothy Gully, Aileen Irwin, Helen DeCew, Kay Park, Betty Sharland and Bobby Huddock. (WIN OLIVER/BUDDY BARKER COLLECTION)

sturdy built Chuck Lauritzen with an Adonis face; or tall lanky Hansen on whom the odds were wagered higher than a dollar to a doughnut among the many 'Scandi-hoovians' present.

Hubert "Abie" Knight took first, George Hansen second and Chuck Lauritzen third. In true Scandinavian tradition, hot milk and rolls were served to all the finishers. A jumping event was also held, probably at the small jump on the Popfly hill at First Lake.

New stars were born as the races continued. Axel Sneis won the cross-country race held in January 1928—the first he had ever entered. Sneis went on to become club champion and Leyland trophy winner in 1929; he was also victorious in the 1930 B.C. cross-country championships at Burns Lake. In March 1928, Finn Fladmark became the first winner of the Leyland Cup, winning both the jumping and cross-country competitions.

Many women also enjoyed cross-country competition. The first race for women, held in April 1928 over a two-mile course, attracted eleven entries. The victor was Doris Parkes with a time of 20:43. Other competitors, in order of finish, were Daisy Bourdon, Millie Kennedy, Kitty Franklin, Dorothy Gully, Aileen Irwin, Helen DeCew, Buddy Barker, Kay Park, Betty Sharland and Bobby Huddock.

Parkes continued to excel in cross-country for the next few years, with victories in the 1929 Hollyburn and 1931 VISKI club races, and second place at the Banff winter carnival. One of the few women to do ski jumping, she had jumps of sixteen and

Vancouver City Championships winners in 1934. Daisy Bourdon (R) came first, and Bertha Haig (Mathews) on the left, was second. Bourdon also won the Pacific Coast championships at Grouse in 1930 and became the Pacific Northwest Champion in 1933 and 1939, B.C. champion in 1933 and the Western Canadian champion in 1934. Haig's victories included the cross-country at the Dominion Championships in Revelstoke in 1931.
(BROWNIE MORRIS/HELEN KALDAHL COLLECTION)

eighteen metres at one event. Most of the few women who jumped at this time were "glider girls," jumping in tandem with an experienced male skier (although no evidence of Hollyburn women doing this has been unearthed). Parkes made her jumps solo.

Writing in the 1935 *Canadian Ski Year Book*, Hollyburn's Daisy Johnson (née Bourdon) describes these early days.

> Most of us knew nothing about wax, but as it was a race, we considered the most important factor was "speed," so on went the candle wax, as thick as we could spread it. Consequently climbing was almost impossible and several girls were to be found grouped together slipping and sliding about, all trying to get up the same place. What fun it was! [. . .] Our harness, which wasn't any too reliable, was tied up with string, so that we shouldn't lose any time with adjustments should our harness come loose. Then too, we carried extra string in our pockets, just as a double safeguard.

Bourdon married ski instructor Gus Johnson. She died of cancer in 1951 at the age of forty-five. Her great competitive success was recognized in 1954 by a trophy sponsored in her name for "any person who has contributed an unusual amount of help toward betterment of skiing in this area."

Initially the only competitions were in cross-country and jumping, but as improved equipment gave the skiers more control of their skis, other races became possible. British ski mountaineer Arnold Lunn is generally credited with setting up the first slalom race at the Palace Hotel in Murrin, Switzerland, in 1922, although earlier slalom races may have been held in Telemarken, Norway. One of the first Canadian slalom races was held on Grouse Mountain in March 1932 and, as a consequence, slalom and downhill were added on the North Shore to the original two disciplines of cross-country and jumping.

The first slalom course on Hollyburn was cut by a work bee November 25, 1934, below the shoulder west of the Romstad's run. In the late 1930s a wider slalom course was cut on the east side of the shoulder, but because it was in the Capilano watershed, it was not used after 1940. The scar is still visible on the southeast slope below the shoulder. Subsequently the Popfly across the lake from Hollyburn Ski Lodge was used for a few years for slalom club races. Slalom's recognition as an Olympic event in 1936 confirmed its acceptance by the skiing world. It became increasingly popular, and women started to compete in slalom about this year. A giant slalom course was also run from the peak of Hollyburn to Sixth Lake, beginning about 1951.

Although die-hard traditionalists such as Verne spurned slalom and downhill as "too effeminate for a skier with real athletic abilities," the skiers voted with their skis. The "two-way-combined" was either downhill and slalom, or jumping and cross-country for men, or slalom and downhill for women. To win the "four-way-combined" —downhill, slalom, cross-country and jumping—was highly prestigious.

Jack Wood speeds down the Romstad's section of the VISKI downhill course on Hollyburn, 1940s. (JACK AND PEGGY PRATT COLLECTION)

All versions of the sport were often hell-bent-for-leather and go-for-it skiing: "Internal injuries were sustained by Iron Man Lew Davis when he schussed the course at an average speed of 60 mph, only to take off on the last turn, shoot 50 feet to the highway, have both skis torn off in a somersault, then smashed into a tree which required him being packed downhill in a sitting position" (*Bushwacker*, May 17, 1939). *The Vancouver Daily Province* on February 28, 1944, reports that "[Bill] Irwin deserved full credit for his win [in the 1944 VISKI Classic] since he finished on top despite a painful injury which resulted when he took a spill on the icy track. He sprained his shoulder but slipped the joint back into place and continued, to finish 22 seconds ahead of second-place Henry Sotvedt." Finn Fladmark's injuries at a 1935 meet in Leavenworth kept him in hospital for ten months. The one fatality of these years at

Hollyburn was in January 1938, when Ben Harstad died of a broken neck after over-balancing on a jump take-off and falling head first onto the hard packed snow.

Brian Creer was another dedicated risk-taker, but he avoided serious injury. At one time he listed thirteen "near misses" in his outdoor activities. An accomplished skier, he won the Dr. J. Curry cup for combined slalom and downhill in 1939, 1941 and 1945, and gained permanent possession of the cup. Decades before visualization became a commonplace of sports psychology, he used this practice effectively to win many races. He also competed in the Canadian national championships in kayaking (C2 500-metre class) for a number of years.

Creer started going up Hollyburn in 1933–34, his last year of high school, and built his cabin, Wander Inn, at this time. He recalls making extra money by packing up loads of 150 pounds for one cent a pound on his spare 150-pound frame. A young lady who met him at the lodge was surprised because she thought that Brian was the name of a pack horse. Now enjoying his waterfront home in West Vancouver, Brian recalls Hollyburn as offering the complete life. He loved its solitude and peace, and often spent Christmas Day on the peak by himself.

But most found bonding with their fellow skiers the main attraction, with many competing successfully in team events. The Hollyburn Pacific Ski Club racing team won the Pacific Coast Ski Team Championship in 1929 in Vancouver. In 1932 the club won the Tupper & Steele Shield inter-club competition for the third time in four years, and thus gained permanent possession of the trophy. The winning team was composed of Bill Brown, Abie Knight, Chuck Lauritzen, Ralph Morris, Eric Twist, Gus Johnson, Bill Hansen, Henry Sotvedt, Irish Beaumont and Tom Mobraaten. The Hollyburn team was particularly successful at Mount Hood in Oregon; a 1933 report states that they won this event four out of the previous five years.

George Bury's memories go back to a time when skiing still centred on the old Nasmyth Mill (a bit of a shack, he says), when he was only eleven. In 1928 he joined the Hollyburn Ski Club, where he recalls great dances followed by nights on fir boughs in the loft of the Ski Camp. He built his own cabin by himself at the age of seventeen from onsite logs, and was one of the group that carried the piano up the hill for the Vancouver Ski Club. Often he stopped for a mug of tea with Pollough Pogue at his cabin near First Lake. His proficiency in downhill and cross-country skiing won him the Pacific Northwest Combined Skiing Championship in 1938.

As skiing developed, new technologies made the task of timing races much easier and more dependable, especially for races that started and finished in different places. In February 1935, the Vancouver Ski Club acquired a portable telephone system with about a mile of wire. A year later, short-wave sets were tested by the club for slalom and downhill racing. In April 1938, a public address system was installed in the new Westlake lodge to help keep spectators informed of events.

▲ First Lake ski jump with the
lower takeoff added, ca. 1940.
(JACK AND PEGGY PRATT
COLLECTION)

◀ Ron Glover on the
First Lake jump, 1950.
(JIM HARMAN COLLECTION)

In the early years, jumping was integral to the ski experience. Until the 1960s it was often the premier event—very unlike today. A succession of jumps at Hollyburn catered to various levels of practice and competition, with most jumps having a relatively short life. The first small jump at the original Old Mill site used the mill's sawdust pile. The first major jump on the North Shore was built at Grouse Mountain in 1926. In 1928 the Hollyburn Swedes—Pearson, Anderson and Irving—built the first significant Hollyburn ski jump near the new ski camp at First Lake, the top of the trestle forty feet (thirteen metres) off the ground. Hemlock, balsam and yellow cedar logs from the location were used, and all work was done by hand. A competition christened a newly constructed jump in January 1930, and a lower platform three metres down was added in the 1930s for times when use of the top platform was unsafe. Ron Glover recalls that they used to dig out the hill to make longer jumps possible—skiers had to have the impact of their landing mitigated by a steep incline, as landing on the flat could result in serious injury. As photographs indicate, equipment and the accepted techniques favoured a relatively upright jumping style, compared

Ski jumpers and their supporters at the foot of the outrun of the West Lake ski jump, 1934.
(WEST VANCOUVER ARCHIVES. HOLLYBURN RIDGE COLLECTION. 010.WVA.HRC)

Mobraaten ski jump, Hollyburn, March 1936.

to modern jumpers whose radical forward lean simulates the shape of an airplane wing. After this jump collapsed under heavy snow in about 1943, another jump built in the same location became the main focus of competition during the late 1940s and early 1950s. When its deterioration made it unusable Fred Burfield blew it up it at the end of the 1954–55 ski season.

The jump built in 1934 on the north shore of West Lake was also a major venue for practice and competition. Designed by Finn Fladmark and built by Hollyburn Pacific Club members Irish Beaumont and Pollough Pogue's son Mickey, its 38 percent grade and eighty-four-metre length made it one of B.C.'s top jumps. In the first competition here on March 11, 1934, Kaldahl won the Edward Mahon trophy with jumps measured at 138 and 136 feet (42.0 and 41.5 metres). As was mentioned earlier, this jump was dismantled when the lodge was moved out of the Brothers Creek watershed in 1938.

The Mobraaten jump, named for the 1936 Olympian Tom Mobraaten, was built in 1936 farther up the mountain. It was used for several competitions, including the Vancouver Ski Zone and city championships in 1939 and the club championships as late as 1953, but dismantled a few years later. Small trestles were also built near Third Lake and Sixth Lake, with a snow jump at Romstad's just west of the old slalom run. With the exception of the West Lake jump, these jumps were relatively small, allowing distances rarely exceeding thirty metres. They favoured fine technicians like Henry Sotvedt rather than the great leapers like Nels Nelsen, who had greater success on Revelstoke's Suicide Hill. But a number of world-class skiers honed their skills at Hollyburn. Only a few of the many stars can be discussed here.

The triumvirate of Tom Mobraaten, Henry Sotvedt and Nordal Kaldahl, known as "The Three Musketeers" and all from the Norwegian silver mining town of Kongsberg, were Hollyburn's elite in the early years. Of the many jumpers who soared with wooden wings on the North Shore mountains, handsome and likeable Mobraaten was perhaps the most skilled. Born in Kongsberg in 1910, he became a member of the Sagrenna Club and won his first jumping event in Norway when he was six. His first pair of skis were staves from a water barrel, rigged up with a homemade harness.

He came to Canada when he was twenty, where a fellow Norwegian, Sigmund Fulsebakke, handcrafted him a pair of touring skis from cedar. He soon established himself as a leader on the local scene by winning the 1933 City Championships, the 1934 and 1938 Western Canadian Championships and the Pacific Northwest Jumping Championships in 1933, 1935 and 1939. He also set a course record for the Kandahar downhill ski race on Grouse Mountain. A keen competitor, he did not allow a fall in a 1936 cross-country race stop him from crossing the finish line a close second, the blood streaming down his face. His accomplishments won him selection as the only Western Canadian skier on the Canadian team that competed at the 1936 Winter Olympics at Garmisch-Partenkirchen, Germany.

But how would he get to the Olympics? Government subsidies and corporate support for such endeavours were virtually non-existent at this time, and international travel was vastly more expensive, in relative terms, than today. His VISKI club members and others had the answer. They pitched in and raised over $600, at a time in the

First Lake ski jump, early 1950s. Hollyburn Lodge is in the centre.
(HOLLYBURN HERITAGE SOCIETY ARCHIVES)

Depression when this would be a reasonable yearly income. Originally, Hans Gunnarson of Revelstoke had also been selected for the Olympic team, but fundraising efforts for him were less successful—he did not go.

At the Olympics, Mobraaten placed ninth in a practice competition with jumps of 236 and 249 feet (71.9 and 75.9 metres). In the actual competition he finished a respectable fourteenth in the jumping in spite of an ankle injury, thirtieth in the combined and fifty-eighth in the eighteen-kilometre cross-country. His jumps of forty-nine and fifty-two metres in the Nordic combined were the sixth best in the jumping section, and he also competed in the downhill and slalom. He also won a spot on the team sent to the 1948 Olympics in St. Moritz, Switzerland.

He remained one of the most durable ski jumpers on the North Shore, often travelling to other competitions. On March 10, 1950, at the age of forty, he set a hill record at Kimberley of 220 feet (67 metres); in the same year he won the B.C. Jumping Championships in Revelstoke. He even tried out (unsuccessfully) for the 1952 Olympics, finishing twelfth in jumping at the Olympic trials in Revelstoke in 1951. His name as winner of the seniors' and veterans' titles frequently appears in the newspapers during the 1950s, including the Western Canadian Ski Championships in 1954 and 1955.

"The Three Musketeers" at a First Lake ski jumping tournament, ca. 1945.
L to R: Henry Sotvedt, Tom Mobraaten, Nordal Kaldahl.
(BROWNIE MORRIS/HELEN KALDAHL COLLECTION)

Henry Sotvedt also competed at the elite level in both Nordic and Alpine events. He won the Western Divisional Championships and Pacific Northwest Championship in cross-country and jumping combined several times. In 1937 he was the top Canadian in Nordic combined at the Canadian National Championships in Banff, and won the U.S.A. National Championships, Veterans' Class, in 1947. Two Skiers Sporting Goods that he and fellow Kongsberger Gus Johnson opened in 1938 at 431 Richards

Scene before the start of the City Championships, March 11, 1934. On the far left, wearing a white headband, is Henry Sotvedt. Nordal Kaldahl, Finn Fladmark and Tom Mobraaten stand next to him. Ommund Ommundsen is in a sweater on the far right.
(BROWNIE MORRIS/HELEN KALDAHL COLLECTION)

Street in Vancouver was the first full-time skiing store in Vancouver. Here a pair of Splitkein skis with lignastone edges could be purchased for $23, or Swiss-model ski boots for $17.50. Although he moved to Wells to work in the mines soon after, the store continued to operate.

After his retirement from active competition he became a technical consultant and spokesman with the Canadian Amateur Ski Association. He organized the first jumping clinics on the West Coast in the early 1950s, initiated the junior jumping program in the high schools and was the first Canadian (with Rolf Dokka) to be certified by the International Ski Federation as an international judge, coach and manager of the Canadian team for the 1964 Olympics. He was also a delegate to the International Ski Federation, and the first Canadian to judge in a European championship. He was involved in the unsuccessful bid to bring the 1980 Olympics to the new resort of Whistler—a bid that, when made again thirty years later, finally met with success.

Nordal Kaldahl, one of the West Coast's most successful competitors, was the third member of "The Three Musketeers." Born in 1903, he had been a member in Norway of the Kongsberg Idretts Forbund (KIF), home club of world champion ski jumpers Sigmund and Burger Ruud, and had competed in the Olympic jumping trials in Europe in 1928. Soon after his arrival in Canada in 1930 he won the Vancouver City Combined Ski Championship in 1931 and 1934, and the Pacific Northwest Championship in Seattle in 1933. During one stretch in 1932 he won five of the nine events he entered; one whole wall of his Vancouver house was full of trophies. Many of Kaldahl's cups and medals are today on display at the renowned Holmenkollen Ski Museum near Oslo, constructed within the base of the jumping trestle.

Perhaps his most remarkable achievement was in 1951, when at the ripe age of forty-eight he won the senior ski jump competition at Mount Baker with jumps of 98 and 101 feet (29.8 and 30.8 metres). He also played an active role in training a new generation of Hollyburn jumpers. He met Helen "Brownie" Morris at Hollyburn in 1931, and they were married (eventually) in 1950. Brownie was an active organizer, serving as secretary for the Vancouver Ski Zone, and subsequently secretary of the Western Canadian Ski Association for five years.

In the next generation Jack Roocroft was one of the leading local skiers. Around 1940, before his first jump, he recalls taking instruction from the experienced jumper Nels Nelsen, who asked him to take a swan-dive position in the air. His background in diving led him to take this advice a trifle too literally, and he ended up doing a face plant in the snow. He overcame this setback to capture the 1947 four-way Western Canadian, the 1950 four-way North American ski championship and the 1954 Central Canadian jumping title. He was a spare for both the 1948 and 1952 Olympics, but lack of funding forced him to stay home. He partially financed some of his international trips by feature articles he wrote for the *Vancouver Sun*.

Injuries and bad luck dogged him. In 1950 he injured the cartilage in his knee during an exhibition jump at Kitsilano. He recovered from this injury, but after a practice jump in Oslo in January 1954 while training for the World Championships in Falun, Sweden, one of his skis froze to the ground in a rut. When he went to move, the ski remained fixed, causing him to fall backwards and badly fracture his right ankle. After his recovery he continued to jump, but although he posted some good results, never dominated as he had earlier. He missed qualifying for the 1956 Olympics, but finished nineteenth in the 1958 Vancouver Empire Stadium international jumping competition, and next year won the four-way Western Canadian championship in Banff. When interviewed for this book in 2007 he was still cracking outrageous jokes and was full of energy, spending his summers sailing and his winters cruising the ski slopes.

Halvor Sellesbach, a VISKI member originally from Norway and coached by his father, burst onto the scene in 1951 at the age of sixteen with the highest points in a Hollyburn jumping competition. He was unbeaten in junior competition that year, and next year started cleaning up in senior ranks. In 1953 he won the Canadian Senior

Jack Roocroft, 1950s.
(JACK ROOCROFT COLLECTION)

Championship, was third in the North American jumping championships in 1954, and won the 1955 Western Canadian Class A Nordic championship with leaps of 225 and 224 feet (67.5 and 67.2 metres). It looked like here at last might be a Canadian jumper who could win that elusive Olympic medal. But after he failed to qualify for the 1956 Olympics he dropped out of sight, some suggesting that he moved back to Norway.

The immediate cause of the decline of jumping on Hollyburn was the deterioration of the wooden jumping trestles; by the mid-1950s no jump on Hollyburn was suitable for competition. Original plans in 1948 had been for a jump at the old West Lake site, although this was later changed to a location closer to First Lake. On May 19, 1951, the Hollyburn Ski Jump Hill Association was started to raise money for a 200-foot (sixty-one metre) jump, the same year in which Grouse Mountain opened a new jump where 180-foot (fifty-five metre) jumps were possible. The push for a new hill may also have been in part a response to the opening of the Hollyburn chairlift.

Plans stagnated for several years but were revived in 1957 with more modest goals. Jack Wood, the municipal forest ranger from 1948 to 1976, persuaded those involved to build a first-class intermediate jump near First Lake rather than go for broke with a world-class one. By the beginning of 1958, $3,500 had been raised by selling shares and raffles, with the municipality of West Vancouver providing matching funds. Jack Wood designed the jump and supervised a crew of four who built the trestle out of mostly donated materials over the summer.

The Jack Pratt Memorial jump was completed east of First Lake near the Grand National Ski Trail in 1958. A sign at the top of this hill now marks its former location. It was named for Jack Pratt, one of Hollyburn's legendary skiers, who was felled by cancer in 1957 at the early age of thirty-seven. Jack is remembered by wife Peggy as a great host, a wonderful fun-loving man.

John Halstead was first down the Jack Pratt jump on January 4, 1959. Signalling the all clear for the first competition on April 4, 1959, was Jack's older son Wayne, with Johan Saldersang taking top honours. But this jump had a short life—no records for competition have been found after April 3, 1960. Alex Swanson states that the municipal forester would never let them cut a decent outrun. In 1962, after Typhoon Freda blew a tree against it, it was no longer used. Swanson recalls the main use of the jump was for sunbathing because there were no bugs up that high. It collapsed in March 1967.

❧

Ski jumping has disappeared from the front pages, and even, for the most part, the sports pages, particularly in Canada. As early as 1937, *The Canadian Ski Year Book*, in an article "The Decline in Ski Jumping," implies that the decline in ski jumping (in Eastern Canada) was inversely related to the growing popularity of downhill and slalom. Although this obituary turned out to be premature, ski jumping by the 1960s had lost much of its allure. Those who wanted thrills and speed could get their kicks out of the longer downhill runs made possible by the new lifts. Jumping competitions are labour intensive; it takes ten people half a day to prepare a thirty-metre hill after a snowfall, and when the machine-groomed runs of the downhill beckon, how many will want to spend that time? Competitions also require a chief judge, a hill chief, a starter, a measurer, hill police, a press helper and an announcer. And ski jumping is

Jack Pratt shows his skill on the Hollyburn slalom run, ca. 1939. Pratt won the 1937 Vancouver City Championship, the Pacific Northwest Cross-country, and was the 1940 North American and the 1947 Western Canadian Four-way Champion. He won the VISKI classic more often than anyone else.
(HUGH "TORCHY" AIKENS PHOTOGRAPH, BUD AND NAOMI MACINNES COLLECTION)

inherently competitive, while most skiers today are in it for the recreation. The skill level needed for competition on today's mammoth jumps is far beyond the comfort level of the average skier.

B.C.'s top skiers most often came from the bigger hills at Princeton or Rossland, and later Whistler, although Grouse did produce Rod Hebron and some others who excelled. Many on the West Coast saw the need for a single club with a high level European coach to unify skiers and competitions. This did not happen and, with a few notable exceptions, Canada's top skiers did not come from the West Coast. No B.C. skiers made the 1956 Olympic team, and only two—cross-country skiers from Camrose, Alberta—came from western Canada.

Canadian training methods remained relatively primitive. While Scandinavians in the 1950s were researching the best aerodynamic positions through the use of wind tunnels, Canadian skiers, particularly jumpers, were still largely self-trained. Any coaching was generally in the form of informal advice from the more to the less experienced. It is amazing that for so long B.C. jumpers could compete with the world's best.

While jumping gradually faded from Hollyburn, downhill races lasted a little longer. The first "tram race," held in February 1952 from the west side of the First Lake jump hill to part way down the Hollyburn chairlift (tram), was won by VISKI Peter Spring. Later tram races were often held higher up the mountain where snow was more abundant. Most races ended by the early 1960s, although when the Cypress downhill area opened in 1974 competition resumed.

The only major competition in the Hollyburn area in recent times was the Canadian cross-country championships in March 1989. This was organized mainly through the local club, the Nordic Racers. Bill Cooper, area manager for the cross-country area, recalls that this stretched the local resources in many ways. So much snow fell one night that the lights shorted out. And to make up the distance for the 50-kilometre race, competitors had to go up to Triangle Lake and back seven times. Hollyburn is not the best locale for this level of competition.

Most sports today have fragmented into different levels. Contemporary competition at Hollyburn and elsewhere has split between the elite competitors, who dedicate their lives to the perfection of their craft and the rewards that might bring, and the weekend warrior, who sees his/her sport as enjoyment and personal challenge. By far the majority of participants fall into the latter category. Cypress Bowl Recreations Limited (CBRL) initiated a Mountain Challenge April 28, 1985, on Hollyburn, with each four-person team including a runner, biker, Nordic skier and alpine skier on the varied elevations. The increased popularity of wilderness trail racing is reflected in the Knee Knackering foot race, a gruelling 50-kilometre grind up and down the mountains from Horseshoe Bay to Deep Cove that passes through Hollyburn on the Baden-Powell trail. Shorter trail races held within Hollyburn attract a variety of gnarly mountain types. The great majority of participants in these competitions are true amateurs, with no ambitions beyond the cultivation of a healthy lifestyle, fulfillment of a personal challenge and catching that guy or girl ahead of them.

CHAPTER 7

Woodland Utopias:
The Cabins of Hollyburn

Here's to all who wish us well—
Hollyburn!
Here's to all who wish us well—
Hollyburn!
Here's to all who wish us well
And all the rest can go to Grouse
Here's to good old Hollyburn!

—TO BE SUNG TO THE TUNE OF
"MADEMOISELLE FROM ARMENTIÈRES"

For many, Hollyburn has served as an oasis to which people could escape from the urban pressures and nourish their souls. This was especially realized through the building of cabins, which required a much greater degree of commitment than just strapping on the boards for the weekend. The heyday of their building was from about 1925 to 1950. Although a number of cabins remain, new private cabins have not been allowed for many years. These are rustic but generally well-built retreats in harmony with their environment, often constructed from materials at hand. They epitomize a fusion of Hollyburn values—self-reliance, rejection of urban materialism, friendship and a co-operative spirit—values which have remained constant to this day. Even today the cabins are well outside the urban grid of running water, electricity and other municipal services.

Cabin life has a unique appeal. For a modest outlay and a lot of sweat, urbanites could in earlier times create a Shangri-La in the woods, a rural retreat just a few hours from their city homes. They are generally built out of logs and quite small in size,

Challenger Inn in the 1980s. Owned by Bert and Jackie Baker for many years, it hosted many memorable social gatherings. (WEST VANCOUVER ARCHIVES. HOLLYBURN RIDGE COLLECTION. C235A WVA. HRC. PHOTO CREDIT: LES FINTA)

often just one room, sometimes with a sleeping loft. Yellow cedar was the preferred wood because of its lasting qualities, but mountain hemlock was more often easier to obtain. While living permanently in the cabins is not permitted, many cherish their getaways for weekends or other times. As Don Nelsen says, "People can have yachts and all those things. But I've got this cabin. It's just heaven." Cabin owners are a smorgasbord of fiercely independent individuals, sharing a love of the wilderness and a disregard for urban formalities. While building of new cabins is now strictly forbidden, owners mostly hang on tightly to the ones they have.

A few of Hollyburn's cabins are on private property, but most are on municipal land. In the early years, when West Vancouver was a low rent outpost for those who could not afford to live in Vancouver, the cabins were a natural extension of the West Vancouver community. But as an affluent lifestyle has become predominant in West Vancouver, the justification of the rustic cabins has at times been subject to intense scrutiny by the municipal administration.

The simple life has attracted many to southwestern B.C., where the relatively benign winters combine with a proximity to urban amenities. On the North Shore, the writer Malcolm Lowry and others took refuge in their shacks in the Deep Cove area, while the Maplewood community group near Second Narrows Bridge lasted until about 1970. Farther up the mountains, Grouse, Seymour and Hollyburn became the sites of extensive cabin communities beginning in the 1920s. While the cabin community on Grouse has now disappeared, and only a few cabins remain on Seymour, Hollyburn has endured, the only cabin community in the Lower Mainland to do so.

Catherine Rockandel, currently President of the Hollyburn Ridge Association, speculates on the reasons for Hollyburn's survival: "Firstly, there were more of them to start with and there was a more active community, so they were better maintained. There was also a strong local and vocal leadership that advocated for their survival and continues to do so through the Hollyburn Ridge Association. . . . You often see one community able to organize while another cannot. The biggest reason is the amount of social capital or trust, collaboration through volunteerism and organized community events, individual leadership, etc. Hollyburn was a community." The collective spirit of the Hollyburn cabin community was fostered also through the presence of the mountain lodges and their activities. In addition there was the supporting infrastructure of transportation, social events and accommodation that the other North Shore mountains did not have to the same extent.

Don Nelsen's rustic retreat "Tickety-Boo," 1993.
(ALEX SWANSON COLLECTION)

▲ Vancouver Ski
Club cabin, 1930s.
(BUD AND NAOMI
MACINNES COLLECTION)

◀ The Swanson family at
The Doghouse in July 1962.
(ALEX SWANSON
COLLECTION)

▲ TOP LEFT: Cabin A/4 belonged to Roy McLaren, Secretary of State in Pierre Trudeau's final cabinet. (WEST VANCOUVER ARCHIVES. HOLLYBURN RIDGE COLLECTION. CA4.WVA.HRC. PHOTO CREDIT: LES FINTA)

TOP RIGHT: Lord Byng students rented the cabin Elby from the Hollyburn Pacific Ski Club, 1944. (BOB TAPP COLLECTION)

▶

Cabin 196 in late spring with the snow off the roof. (ALEX SWANSON COLLECTION)

Replacing logs at the Lidster cabin, August 1964. L to R: Kjell Karlson,
Doug Sparks and Joe Lidster. (ALEX SWANSON COLLECTION)

Many of the Hollyburn cabin owners have high profiles in the community and beyond, which may also have helped Hollyburn to survive. For example, long-time Hollyburner and cabin owner Jack Harman received the Order of Canada in 1996 for his accomplishments as a sculptor, painter and teacher at the Vancouver School of Art and the Emily Carr College of Art and Design. His first foundry, started in 1962 at his home in Lynn Valley, produced many landmarks in Vancouver and elsewhere, including the "Miracle Mile" statue of Roger Bannister and John Landy at the PNE. The large foundry he established in 1982 cast the statue of sprinter Harry Jerome in Stanley Park, the "Themis, Goddess of Justice" figure at the B.C. Law Courts, Queen Elizabeth on a horse at the Parliament Buildings in Ottawa, and a number of others.

Others helped create the community through their unique brand of innovative activities. Bob Tapp's "History of the Hollyburn Western Telephone Company (sort of)" a part of which is quoted here, provides a window into some past activities of the convivial group that still endures at Hollyburn:

This unique "company" operated in the cabin area in the 1950s and early '60s with the head office at the "Ladies and Escorts" beer parlour at the Olympic Hotel in North Vancouver. Directors paid their dues in 10-cent glasses of beer, and the company's mission statement was simple: "We are not a public company and it's nobody's business what business we are doing being in business."

The physical plant of the business was started when Bert Baker (Challenger Inn) located some hand-crank, battery-operated telephones at a closed mine, and a director's assessment bought the galvanized steel wire and climbing spurs. Utilizing the spurs to climb trees, enthusiastic cabin owners strung a single line from Mel Leslie's Sky Tavern to John Halstead's Rock Mount Manor with branches at Bob Tapp's Red Pony Taproom, Pete Cherry's Ranger Station, John Eaves, Bert Baker's Challenger and Pete Berntzen's Viking, Jack Rockandel's Staggering Arms and others. Bert Baker ran Norm Deacon's tows in the Hollyburn area, so the line was extended to Westlake, allowing them to discuss the operation of the eight tows.

The cabin may be small but it is snug and cozy. Bob and Greta Tapp, with their family at Homenkollen, February 2008. (BOB TAPP COLLECTION)

With an interconnect at the Ranger Station it was possible to reach the outside world. Bert Baker and his companions called Sun Valley to make reservations one year, and another time it was used to save a heart attack victim, but mostly it was used to call a friend to bring another bottle to the party when supplies were running low, or to find out where the dance was.

The telephone lines have long gone, but something of the same community spirit continues with the present cabin owners when they get together for the Logger's Day Festival, cabin walks and various activities for children, such as lantern-making.

The cabins might be said to have their roots in West Vancouver's early role as a summer recreation area. In 1918 Jack Cruickshank and his friends bought a large tent and pitched it near the waterfront, where they spent the summer and commuted to their work in Vancouver. They called their tent the "Kennel," and themselves the "Hounds." All had maroon turtleneck sweaters with blue and white trim, with each sweater sporting a large yellow letter of the Hounds' name. At this time, a number of similar camps of both young men and women and families created a community on the waterfront where good fellowship made for relaxed times.

Cabin life farther up the mountain began even earlier. Trappers and others whose work or interests took them to the outdoors built cabins from the early 1900s. George Marr bought fifty-eight acres (23.5 hectares) and built a cabin in 1904 about where the former Hollyburn chairlift crossed 27th Street. Pollough Pogue noted in May 1922 that Joe Gojack had a "hermitage" a thousand feet up Black Mountain. Several cabins were built around First Lake before Hollyburn Ski Camp; Pogue noted in August 1923 that there was already a cabin at First Lake complete with stove and bunks. Laurence Greig built a cabin in the summer of 1925 at Sixth Lake to which he brought groups of young boys to whom he taught woodcraft. Many of the Scandinavian skiers and woodsmen who arrived in Canada in the 1920s were proficient cabin builders who crafted exquisite cabins from the yellow cedar (cypress) that abounded at higher levels. Oscar Pearson built twenty-one cabins himself, and Gus Johnson seventeen. These were mostly built on spec and sold at $300 or so each. Some continued to be rented into the '70s. Jim Harman recalls buying a cabin with three friends for $250 in 1943, an affordable price for a young working single.

The growth of the cabin community accelerated after 1929 when, during the Depression, the growing number of unemployed men constructed much needed cheap accommodation. While most were weekenders, a number of young men such as Jack Pratt, Bud James, Eddie Oakley and Fred Burfield were permanent residents. The number grew to 250 by 1936, and perhaps as many as 300 by World War II.

Ommund Ommundsen (left) and Finn Fladmark enjoy their
"Poor Man's Delight" at Eilif Haxthow's cabin on Hollyburn, 1926.
(EILIF HAXTHOW COLLECTION)

The first cabins often used some of the two-by-twelve boards from the flume. Many of these were shacks, glorified tree forts built by adolescent boys, and were generally less weather resistant than the later log cabins. The early cabins have long returned to the forest, but many of the later cabins were more durable. These were often built from logs that had been cut to create the ski runs, with roofs fashioned from shakes split from shingle bolts. About forty trees were needed for a small cabin.

The most active area in the early days was on the way up to the Hollyburn Ski Camp at First Lake. Charlie McGowan, Tom Gibson, Ian Elger and Charlie McMillan were some of the West Vancouver lads who built the early cabins. The names were as colourful as the owners: Cabin du Bois, Staggering Arms, Lost Weak End, Kwityer Belyakin, Hellzapoppin, Tryundfindit and Valhalla, to name a few. In the Bowlers' cabin on the old flume trail, each of the four residents wore black bowler hats. Don Nelsen recalls that in the years following World War II the mountain was full of activity both summer and winter, with rows of cabins east and west from the top of the chairlift. Many cabin owners brewed their own refreshments, called by Eilif

▲ Finn Fladmark built this
cabin, Skiesta, in about 1934.
(BOB TAPP COLLECTION)

◀ First Aid cabin at
Romstad's, 1940s.
(BURFIELD FAMILY
COLLECTION)

▶ Jim Graham and Don Fraser built The Woodhouse in 1932.
(JIM GRAHAM COLLECTION)

▼ BOTTOM LEFT: Te Anua Nua. One of the few cabins where the log work is vertical.
(ALEX SWANSON COLLECTION)

BOTTOM RIGHT: Siggi's Hideout built with logs by Gerry Hardman.
(ALEX SWANSON COLLECTION)

Haxthow and others "Poor Man's Delight." Bill Prior, owner of Misty Manor, ran a clandestine still that produced such good liquor that he sometimes traded a bottle for a bottle of scotch. The pervasive atmosphere was one of healthy exercise, light-hearted fun and good fellowship.

Bears were a common sight in past years in the cabin area, with many of the cabin owners coming up on a weekend to find that a bear had broken into their cabin and scattered the food. Joe Stewart tells how, for his cabin, it used to happen especially in the spring, when the bears came out of hibernation and the snow was high enough around the cabin for them to be at roof level. They could then pry open a shutter, break the glass and clamber in. Les Finta, who hiked the trails regularly, had frequent encounters with bears but said that they almost always ran away when they spotted him. The bears are obviously still there, although they seem to be more elusive than in earlier times. Especially in the fall when the berries are ripe, one finds considerable bear scat on the trails. With their excellent noses, dogs can offer some early warning, but if they annoy the bear and the bear charges the dog, the dog will run back to its owner for protection. Not a good situation. One often hears dogs with their "bear bells" tinkling on the mountain trails. Recently, Veronica Hatch came upon a huge scat filled with blueberries, still "reeking warm," next to her cabin, and suddenly found her dog Clio tugging at the leash to track the animal. She made sure to keep the dog on a tight lead. From time to time, the municipality posts signs warning hikers that bears are in the area. A few of the cabin owners say they have regular visits, especially if they put out bird seed for the whiskey jacks.

Cabin owners have always traded tips on forest living. Through their newsletter, *The Ridgerunner*, they give one another advice on dealing with mice, repairing outhouses and keeping down the humongous flying ants that appear each spring. Of course there is always the sharing of recipes. Especially prized are those that one can begin in the city and finish quickly on the cookstove in the cabin. Here is one from Silvie Keen for Sweet and Sour Pork:

AT HOME

Meat: mix together 2 tbsp soy sauce, 2 tbsp sherry, a few drops of sesame oil and 1 tbsp cornstarch. Add 1 lb. of cubed pork, toss to coat, place in a baggie and refrigerate.

Sauce: mix together 1 tbsp soy sauce, 1/2 cup sugar, 1/3 cup vinegar (rice or white wine vinegar), 1/2 cup water, 2 tbsp tomato paste, 1 tbsp cornstarch and place in a leak-proof container.

Veggies: a broccoli crown cut into florets, 6-10 mushrooms halved, and a carrot peeled and sliced on the diagonal. Pack it all up along with a knob of fresh ginger and/or a couple of garlic cloves.

AT THE CABIN

Rice: 2 parts water to 1 part rice, salt and a few drops of oil. Bring to a good boil, cover and reduce heat to very low. Cook 20 minutes, with no peeking. Remove from the heat, let it sit for another 5 minutes and then remove the lid and fluff with a fork.

Meat: while the rice is cooking, heat a skillet or wok over medium-high heat. Add oil, then throw in some sliced fresh ginger and/or garlic. Give it a stir and then add the meat. Let it brown a little and then give it a stir and stir-fry for 5 minutes. Now would be a good time to fluff the rice. Add the veggies, keep on stir-frying until the meat is cooked through and the vegetables are crisp-tender. Give the sauce a good shake to remix and then add to the stir-fry. Bring to a boil and serve over the rice.

Originally, anyone built anywhere, the spirit of pioneering free enterprise trumping environmental and other concerns, but both the municipality and most of the cabin owners realized that the unchecked frontier spirit could not last forever. While the West Vancouver Council wanted some control over activities in its jurisdiction, the cabin owners desired a certain amount of protection. An article by James McLaughlin in about 1931 notes that young thieves had been breaking into cabins, stealing "blankets, cooking utensils, food and practically everything necessary to the cabin in the woods." Cabin owners formed a watch committee in response.

New regulations by the municipality required cabins to be within a defined area, built only of logs, with proper sanitation to be observed. J.E. Walker was appointed a building inspector October 3, 1932, but left soon after, as his efforts to collect lease fees (he was paid on commission) met with little success. In 1932, with about 200 cabins in use, Scotty Finlayson was hired to supervise and collect the lease fees of ten dollars for the District of West Vancouver. He was paid a regular salary of twenty-five dollars a month, and in his report on June 1, 1933, reports that fifty-three cabins were paying the ten dollar fee. Many others did not. As Alan Jessup writes, ". . . when an inspector approaches a cabin to levy the annual tax, it is in most cases empty. Of course the fire may still be burning and a kettle simmering on the hearth, but the inhabitants are missing."

Inspectors or rangers were an integral part of Hollyburn's development. They not only monitored cabin activity and collected fees; they also removed dead animals from creeks, provided first aid, dealt with overly friendly bears and taught many people to ski. Some, such as Jack Wood, also provided valuable advice on ski projects. Their presence today is missed. For the past number of years, Les Finta was on the mountain as the "assistant ranger." An expert skier himself, he often helped skiers who went out of bounds and became lost. When the temperatures dropped, he also threw ashes on some of the steeper sections of the trails so that visitors up for the day (often in running shoes) would not fall on the icy surface. He was a mine of experience about the mountain and helped many of the cabin owners with repairs to the cabins. It requires a good deal of expertise to remove rotten logs and replace them with sound ones.

During World War II access to Hollyburn was restricted. All "enemy aliens" were barred from Hollyburn Ridge to protect the district's water supply from sabotage. All persons climbing the ridge had to use one of two trails—22nd Street to Hollyburn, or the 15th Street trail to Westlake. Especially during the period following Pearl Harbor, when many feared a Japanese invasion, the visible area of lights was reduced to a narrow slit and held facing the ground to prevent it being visible from above.

After World War II, the Cold War atmosphere led some to look to the cabin area as a place of refuge in case of nuclear attack. Jack Wood, the municipal forest ranger at this time, was one of a number who suggested at a civil defence meeting that the cabins could be useful for possible rapid evacuation. And how many people could be shoehorned into two or three hundred cabins?

After the chairlift burned down in 1965, Hollyburn became a largely forgotten area. West Vancouver Council began phasing out the private cabins, allowing no new construction; between 1963 and 1973 forty-one cabins disappeared. It was the completion of the Cypress Bowl Highway that revived interest in this area. Some feared the new road would lead to an uncontrolled increase in the number of cabins. To forestall this possibility, the West Vancouver Council adopted a bylaw requiring a two acre (one hectare) minimum site size for any new cabins on private land. In 1973 they put a freeze on the transfer of permits for cabins on municipal land. Some West Vancouverites felt they were subsidizing the lifestyles of outsiders, as many of the cabin owners were not from West Vancouver.

The potential threat to their way of life galvanized the cabin owners into action. The Hollyburn Ridge Association was incorporated in 1973 with a constitution declaring the following objectives:

1. The protection and preservation of the Hollyburn cabin area;

2. That we promote the recreational use and public access to the Hollyburn Ridge area;

3. To negotiate with all levels of government to encourage and promote the aims and objectives of the Hollyburn Ridge Association.

"Kwityer Belyakin" after its foundation collapsed, September 1974. Despite efforts to make repairs, the cabin was dismantled. Remnants of the Jack Pratt Memorial Jump are visible on the left. (ALEX SWANSON COLLECTION)

This group, which has continued to the present day, in many ways continues the political function of the earlier ski clubs, with some social activity thrown in.

The next years were stressful, as cabin owners fought for their survival. In about March 1974 West Vancouver Council established a committee, comprising three councillors and three representatives from the Hollyburn Ridge Association, to develop a land and recreational use policy for Hollyburn Ridge.

The Hollyburn Ridge Committee Report was presented to West Vancouver Council by chairman and alderman Donald Lanskail on May 3, 1976. This report recognized the legitimacy of cabins, although it opposed new construction. In addition, any extensive renovations would require municipal approval. A further report in March 1981 states that "there should be a natural phasing out policy adopted by Council, which might take twenty years or more." The February 1983 issue of the Hollyburn Ridge Association's newsletter *The Ridge Runner* communicates a sense of crisis and the need for positive action. "We are alarmed and dismayed at the large number of cabins that are not receiving sufficient care to keep them in good condition. . . . If we don't try to keep *all* of the remaining cabins in good condition, the W.V. District may slowly pick the cabins off, one by one."

A degree of stability was achieved when, beginning in 1984, West Vancouver issued transferable five-year "permits-to-occupy" to all cabin owners. The Ridge Association also negotiated successfully with Wayne Booth of Cypress Bowl Recreations Ltd. to make available some overnight parking spaces in the cross-country parking lot and blocks of four cross-country ski passes for a reasonable $125, rising to $257 by 2008.

The Bread Lady's cabin. In 1936, Mrs. Hughes had this unusually large cabin built for her across from the Forks Store to support herself and her son during the difficult days of the Depression. The cabin was destroyed years ago. (ALF CHARBONNEAU COLLECTION)

This temporary calm was shattered by a new sense of crisis as the next decade dawned. By 1990 only a few cabins at Seymour remained, and on June 30, 1991, the remaining thirty Grouse Mountain cabin owners had their permits to occupy cancelled. The Hollyburn Ridge Association urged its members to "use it or lose it," as many owners were getting long in the tooth and allowing their cabins to deteriorate. A 1992 open letter from the Ridge Association's executive expressed concern: "We believe the long range program is to eliminate cabins by attrition and as cabins fall into disrepair they will be torn down." The proposal for a golf course in the area immediately to the west of the cabins, although it failed, added to their concerns (see below, pp. 159–63).

In spring 1994 negotiations with the District of West Vancouver began for a new permit to occupy. In 1997 the permits were ready. The preamble to the agreement states that "West Vancouver recognizes that the Hollyburn Ridge cabins are part of a valuable and unique wilderness area within its boundaries." It has set the tone for a period of relative peace for the cabin owners with permits, although their lives are not without stress. Problems owing to the proximity of a large urban population persist. Eighteen break-ins occurred in February and March 2002, and for a time a squatter lived in a tent across and down from the last switch-back. Monitoring cabins to ensure they are kept up to a standard is an ongoing process, but generally stability has been achieved.

In the fall of 2004 the District of West Vancouver, with the participation of the Hollyburn Ridge Association, inspected each cabin within the Municipal Cabin Area. Catherine Rockandel, President of the Hollyburn Ridge Association, describes the process, summarized here:

> One or more representatives from the Hollyburn Ridge Association and the District of West Vancouver inspected each cabin. At the conclusion of the inspections, each cabin was discussed and a consensus reached regarding the deficiencies (if any), the repairs needed, and the amount of time the repairs could reasonably be expected to be completed.
>
> The cabins were split into three categories:
>
> 1. Those that were in good repair were issued a new five year permit.
> 2. Cabins that needed some repair received a two year permit but received a letter outlining the mandatory repairs and a completion date. . . .
> 3. Cabins that are in such a deteriorated condition or having situations involving substantial permit violations will not have their permit renewed by the District.

Westlake cabins, 1993.
(ALEX SWANSON COLLECTION)

Norm Deacon on the porch of his Hollyburn cabin in Deaconsville, late 1940s.
His Westlake cabin was expropriated by the District of West Vancouver in 2006.
(BERT BAKER COLLECTION)

Because of the stringent inspections, a great deal of work was required on most of the cabins. A number of owners found it necessary to group together to helicopter in yellow cedar logs to replace those that were rotting, and many were kept busy summer and winter working to bring their cabins up to the new standard. Ten cabins lost their permits between 2006 and 2008. A process to re-permit the cabins is presently under way. In 2008 there were 108 left. Although slow attrition continues, threats to the viability of the cabin community as a whole have been allayed. The new permits to occupy went out in 2004 for the period from January 1, 2005, to December 31, 2009.

As a result of all the recent work required, cabins that used to sell for a relatively low price can now sell for $30,000 to $70,000, and can be sold on the open market. It seems a high price to pay for a small cabin, and these are "cabins" in the true sense of the word—no million dollar Whistler chalets here. They are often no more than 200 to 300 square feet, most with old-style single-pane windows. In winter it can take an airtight stove going full-blast to keep the occupants warm. Anyone owning a cabin is well aware of the work needed for its maintenance, which is considerable without any electric tools. And of course there is always the snow to be shovelled off the roof in winter to prevent the roofs from collapsing. Cabin owners often have to shovel their roofs twenty to thirty times during a winter of heavy snowfall. Yet the cabins, if they are well kept up, offer cozy retreats where the urban dweller can escape to a simpler time.

&

Well yes, mostly true, but as with many Hollyburn matters, new wrinkles continually appear. Nine cabins that were not part of the Hollyburn group were on two pieces of private property of ten and fifteen acres associated with the former Westlake Lodge, built thirty to fifty years earlier. The District of West Vancouver had bought this land from Dianne Clark and Ken Harper in 1990. In order to reduce its purchase price, the District gave the former owners a permit to rent the cabins for two five-year terms. The renters themselves have no permits to occupy, so do not fall under the same rubric as the Hollyburn Ridge Association's cabins. But as most of the renters were long term, they acquired a feeling of entitlement.

After the expiration of the permit in 2000, the renters tried unsuccessfully to achieve similar status to those enjoyed by the Hollyburn Ridge Association cabins. Some, like Alvin Stephenson, fixed up their cabins, spending much time and effort. Bradley Shende states that he has spent $70,000 on maintenance and materials. In general, though, the cabins were poorly maintained shacks, and stories have circulated that some of the tenants were unfriendly and even abusive to hikers and others who wandered by their neighbourhood. As no rents had been paid after the expiration of the permits in 2000, some cabins had become occupied by squatters. In December 2006 the cabin residents were told they would have to clear out, and on June 6, 2007, the District posted notices telling occupants to remove their belongings by August 13. In early October 2007 all the cabins except one were torn down and burned.

The one surviving cabin was used by Barry Deacon, whose father Norm built many of the earliest tows in the area, and built this cabin in about 1980. Crafted of yellow cedar, the cabin is in excellent shape, and will likely be kept standing. But the locks have been changed while the District decides on their plans. Rumours circulate that the cabin will serve as the nucleus for a youth camp. In any case, Barry can now

only view it from the outside and hope that the inevitable deterioration of an unoc-
cupied cabin during the winter will not be too great. He would like to use and care
for the cabin until the District comes up with some concrete plans. Although he and
the other former residents are upset at losing their hideaways, they had no legal basis
to remain in them. They may, like Barry, have built the cabins and maintained them
for decades, but they were on private land.

Nevertheless, for the cabin owners with permits-to-occupy from West Vancouver,
there is a sense of real pleasure in having a little piece of wilderness so close to the city.
The upkeep may require a massive commitment and a strong back, but there is something quite wonderful about being on the mountain in the fresh air surrounded with
mountain hemlock and yellow cedar and hearing the whoosh of the ravens as they fly
overhead through the canopy. Such people regard it as a privilege to be part of the
mountain.

CHAPTER 8

More Forays into Logging

If a tree falls in the forest . . .

Hollyburn's magnificent forests and proximity to a large urban centre make it ripe for commercial enterprise as well as recreation. Much of its history has been a struggle among groups with very different visions—whether it is those who want to retain its pristine integrity, those who want to make a buck or those who need to use its water resources. In more recent years these struggles have often grown keen and bitter.

In 1908, F.H. and Annetta Heeps of Los Angeles acquired seven timber licenses totalling about 3,500 acres (1,417 hectares) on Hollyburn for $137,000. This meant that they owned the timber but not the land, most of which was owned by the District of West Vancouver. In 1928, Heeps expressed concern that the Municipality of West Vancouver had leased Lot 1148 at First Lake to the Hollyburn Ski Camp on land that he had leased from the provincial government. Some at the Hollyburn Ski Camp were building cabins from trees taken from his lease. In compensation he received an eighth license on three municipal lots.

George Bury states that in about 1935, some Japanese interests also acquired some timber rights on Hollyburn and started to build a road. Worried that their pristine skiing would be compromised, Bury teamed up with his friend George Smith and sent a telegram to Premier Duff Patullo to express their concerns. Much to everyone's surprise, they were granted an interview with the premier. They travelled to Victoria and apparently convinced him of the imminent danger to skiing; the timber rights were exchanged for rights elsewhere.

But Heeps was still around. On May 23, 1938, he appeared at a West Vancouver council meeting stating his plans for logging his timber leases on Hollyburn Ridge. Why now? Could it be that, with the Depression still deeply entrenched, he felt the hunger for jobs would make the municipalities more amenable to cutting a deal? Or perhaps he anticipated that the looming war would increase the value of the timber? Or was this, as many expected, all a bluff to pressure the government for an exchange for more marketable timber? While the exact nature of his game is hard to ascertain, there is little doubt that the feeling of many that they were being manipulated by a Yankee sharpie had some basis.

Heeps began a logging road up the Ridge to the 2,200-foot (670-metre) level in June 1938, attempting to portray himself as a benefactor opening up the area to public use. A newspaper article dated July 16 stated that he was planning to take out shingle bolts the next week from the timber leases he owned on Hollyburn Ridge. A long-time Hollyburn supporter and at this time West Vancouver's reeve James Leyland was especially incensed, firing off telegrams to the Hon. Wells Gray, the minister of lands, and to the Vancouver Board of Trade. Vancouver alderman Halford Wilson reported on August 10 after a visit to Hollyburn that "Present logging operations are a disgrace. It is a crime the way beautiful slopes are being destroyed." Others were attracted by the commercial possibilities at a time in the Depression when few such existed. In anticipation of development, Jim Sambrook, owner of the Forks store, constructed an eighteen-metre foundation for a bunkhouse to house the workers expected on the project (the Heeps road went right by his door). Sambrook's bunkhouse was never completed.

At a meeting on July 29, which included Vancouver mayor George Miller, West Vancouver reeve Leyland, ridge inspector Scotty Finlayson and a number of others from the Parks Board, Board of Trade, and other organizations, the consensus was that the timber was mostly hemlock, larch and amabilis fir, which would not be profitable to log at that time. The more valuable western red cedar was scattered and expensive to log. The steep road needed for access and the difficulty of winter logging made the enterprise of doubtful profitability (although Heeps at this point had virtually finished his access road). Those present agreed that this area would make much better sense as a park. Logging would ruin its recreational value.

Wildly fluctuating estimates of the amount of timber reflected the agendas of the

Bob Tapp plays bagpipes on Sambrook's bunkhouse
foundation at the Forks, 6:30 a.m. Easter, 1946.
(BOB TAPP COLLECTION)

different parties. The minister of lands hired timber cruiser Lloyd Rogers of the
Capilano Timber Company to investigate the matter. While Heeps contended there
was as much as 100 million feet on these leases, Rogers reported 29.3 million feet of
merchantable timber, made up of 33 percent hemlock, 54 percent balsam, 5 percent
red cedar, and 8 percent yellow cedar. West Vancouver did not have the money to take
over the area, and in any case its residents were only a small percentage of the Hollyburn users. Vancouver regarded it as a provincial matter. And while the province was
concerned, it was unwilling to pay Heeps the $125,000 he requested as his price for
disappearing. And so it went.

The ski club members, outraged at Heeps' threat to the sanctity of their weekend
paradise, campaigned vigorously against his plans. The newly formed Hollyburn Promotion Ski Committee proposed that the provincial government transfer to the Hollyburn Park Association 3,200 acres (1,295 hectares) of crown lands lying on and con-
tiguous to Hollyburn Ridge in perpetuity for park purposes. A meeting at the original
Hotel Vancouver on October 20, 1938, unanimously supported the plan, and a dele-
gation proceeded to Victoria where the premier and several of his cabinet received
them. But the provincial government remained noncommittal. Reeve Leyland with
councillors Gisby, Edgar and Fiddes, and chief forester E.C. Manning attended the
opening of the Vancouver Ski Club's new clubhouse November 12, 1938, but no
provincial politicians appeared.

The provincial government soon became more supportive. Wells Gray, minister of lands for the provincial government, became an advocate for a park encompassing the North Shore mountains from Hollyburn to Indian River. The initial cost of up to $125,000 was to be financed by a bond issue backed by its revenue-producing possibilities. Plans included a $12,000 chalet and sports centre on the northern shore of Yew Lake. But these plans foundered on conflicting interests and the reluctance of the different levels of government to provide financial backing. North and West Vancouver were especially concerned with ensuring that any development did not jeopardize a reliable water supply.

Confronted with a difficult problem, the provincial government took the normal government action: commission a report. Well-known Hollyburner James Sinclair (Rhodes Scholar, in 1940 elected a Liberal MP, and later Margaret Trudeau's father) was commissioned by the Honourable W.J. Asselstine, minister of trade and industry, to report on the possibility of establishing a provincial park extending from Hollyburn to Mount Seymour, and preparing a long-term plan for the development of ski runs and hiking trails. Sinclair was given a two-month leave of absence from his position as secretary to Asselstine to prepare this report. He took advantage of this time to visit the ski resorts of Mount Rainier, Mount Hood, Sun Valley, Banff and Sunshine.

His report, dated March 1, 1939, suggested that a park encompassing the North Shore mountains was both feasible and desirable, and that the provincial government, with far greater resources than the small communities of West Vancouver and North Vancouver, should assume responsibility for the considerable costs of development— after all, most people who came to the North Shore for recreation were from Vancouver. He suggested that the park include the Cypress Creek watershed, but exclude the Brothers Creek and Nelson Creek drainages, which in any case were marginal recreational areas. He had a benign view of logging, stating that, because any logging would be only the selective extraction of the more valuable red and yellow cedar, it would open up the area for skiing, and would not affect the view from Vancouver.

Others were less convinced that logging was so benign. On July 6, 1939, a rally held at the Hotel Vancouver pressured the government to reveal its intentions for the Hollyburn area. Fifteen hundred people took part at the meeting chaired by James Sinclair. Included were chief forester E.C. Manning, George Vance, commissioner of North Vancouver, and reeve J.B. Leyland of West Vancouver. Enthusiastic support was expressed for a winter playground at their doorstep, providing a local alternative to the long trip to Mount Baker. The vision of a park encompassing the whole range of the North Shore mountains—Hollyburn, Grouse and Seymour—fired the imaginations of many outdoors enthusiasts.

To establish a park, an agreement for West Vancouver to hand over the land to the province was necessary. But West Vancouver was reluctant to give up control of

Premier John Hart and other government dignitaries during a trip to Hollyburn Ridge, April 27, 1944. (CITY OF VANCOUVER ARCHIVES 1184-506, JACK LINDSAY PHOTO)

its land until it had a guaranteed water supply from other sources and funding for the necessary infrastructure. The estimated cost of obtaining an equivalent supply of water from the Water District was $20,000. In addition it would be necessary to pump water to the higher levels of the municipality, currently fed by gravity from high intakes. Faced with these contentious issues, the provincial government decided instead to limit its resources to developing Mount Seymour as a recreational area, where a provincial park had already been established, and no watershed or other issues muddied the waters.

At this point, Heeps took his chance to get back into the picture. In April 1940 he sold his logging interests on Hollyburn to E.E. Olson's Cypress Creek Logging Company for $60,000; by June, sixteen men were cutting timber, with the camp based on the Old Mill site. War apparently had made the hemlock more marketable. Olson argued there would be little effect on skiing, as most of the logging would be to the west of the skiing area. The loggers began working on a forty-acre block about half a mile to the west of the Old Mill, but the purity of their intentions was soon questioned. On a trip to Black Mountain in the fall of 1940, the BC Mountaineering Club found that "logging operations had so altered the appearance of the country that the trails were lost in a hopeless maze."

Little happened for the next two years, but in November 1943 the Hollyburn Logging Company contracted with Cypress Creek Logging for the licenses, felling 40,000 to 50,000 feet of logs daily. The scene, according to reporter Eric Lyons, was one of "devastation," as logging proceeded at top speed to take advantage of the high wartime prices. Trees nearly five hundred years old were felled, with cutting planned at the rate of 12 million feet annually. Logging at this time encroached to only a few hundred yards west of the trail to the skiing area.

In late 1943 provincial lands minister Wells Gray and the Municipality of West Vancouver moved to expropriate the land needed for a park and to protect the West Vancouver water supply from the effects of logging. On April 27, 1944, B.C. premier John Hart made a symbolic hike to the top of Hollyburn Ridge. The Hollyburn Forest Conservation plan set aside 3,500 acres (1,417 hectares) of timber land on the crest of Hollyburn Ridge as a park reserve under Order-in-Council 1423. But it was not formally dedicated or declared, or put on map reservations for parks. No park just yet, but at least the area was preserved from logging. Or so it was thought.

An exchange of Heeps' Hollyburn timber, valued at $100,000, was arranged with Elk Bay, north of Campbell River on Vancouver Island. The exchange was based on volume rather than quality, with the low-grade Hollyburn timber exchanged for high-grade fir. While the Hollyburn timber and Elk Bay licenses were both assessed at 45 million feet, by 1970 it was ascertained that 55 million feet had been taken from the new lease, and it was still being operated. Certainly not a bad deal for the Heeps logging interests.

The land in West Vancouver below the 1,200-foot (366-metre) level is mostly privately owned, with British Pacific Properties the largest owner from 1931 on. In the 1940s British Pacific Properties reduced their planned house lot size from 1.25 acres (0.51 hectares) to half or less, and removed trees to clear views and open lots for development. In 1947, Goodwin Johnson Jr., whose father had been manager of Capilano Timber Limited from 1917 to 1930, seized on a good business opportunity and started logging British Pacific Properties land at the top of Taylor Way. The industrious Mr. Johnson, awarded the title of Mother Cedar Tree by the Squamish band for supplying them with logs for their first longhouse, logged off a number of areas in the eastern portion of British Pacific Properties, as well as working his way west, mostly on land owned by the British Pacific Properties, to just above and beyond Horseshoe Bay. Much of this was second- or third-growth fir, although some old growth remained.

The Wells Gray ski run on Hollyburn, early 1940s. Named after
Arthur Wellesley Gray, minister of lands for the B.C. provincial government
1933–41, in recognition of his efforts to protect the forests on the
North Shore mountains. (CHUCK AND JUNE GILLRIE COLLECTION)

The resulting cleared areas became subdivisions, the revenue from logging often paying for the lot. But the clear-cuts and piles of slash left behind by Johnson's efforts
were ugly blemishes on the landscape and a dangerous fire hazard.

The company sold thousands of telephone poles to Naugle Poles in Chicago, with
the short ones going to Saskatchewan and Manitoba. They also sold poles for docks,
piers and telephone poles "from Sumatra and Singapore to Australia and Iceland."
With a staff of up to 130 workers, Johnson logged the British Pacific Properties up to
Brothers Creek's lower falls, and down to Rabbit Lane. The forty acres of Glenmore
subdivision was done as a single block. The forests that became Cedardale, Altamount,
Westmount and Bayridge subdivisions and the area south of Eagle Lake fell before

his company's advance. He finished logging in 1953, having removed approximately 15 million board feet of lumber: 45 percent hemlock, 35 percent balsam, 10 percent red cedar and 10 percent yellow cedar.

By the early 1950s reports that logging was accelerating and that West Vancouver was ringed by 3,000 acres (1,214 hectares) of tinder dry logging slash, a fire waiting to happen, were raising concerns. A slash burn in 1951 surged out of control and burned about sixty acres (twenty-four hectares), and in June the next year 400 to 500 acres (162 to 203 hectares) of slash burned along Sisters Creek. As has happened too often, by the time the public outcry caused action, the deed was done, and, for better or worse, the shape of residential West Vancouver was determined. With nature's typical forgiving generosity, trees have now grown to replace a good number of those cut down, and some of the original beauty has returned.

CHAPTER 9

Tows and Transportation

༷

On one of these marvellous moonlight nights a handsome and
graceful young man's strong arm guided me over the ice and this
clumsy novice became a Sonja Heini for the moment. And on
December 7 one year, with no snow in sight, the impatient skiers trying
to pass the time dared Ted Yard and I to swim the lake. We accepted
the challenge, we swam and we reaped the reward, which was an apple
pie homemade by the famous pie maker of the mountain, Vic Wills.

—NAOMI MACINNES, "A SENTIMENTAL JOURNEY" (1976)

With the opening of the Lions Gate Bridge in 1938, road access to Hollyburn became much easier, as did access farther up Hollyburn Mountain via (ironically) the road that Heeps had built to exploit the timber. After the first rope ski tow in Western Canada opened on Grouse Mountain in November 1938, a number of ambitious proposals for tows were floated. At a West Vancouver council meeting on March 27, 1939, John Daly proposed a ski tow from Romstad's to the Hollyburn shoulder. This was not installed. At another council meeting on May 22 of that year, Hamilton Bridge Western Limited proposed a more ambitious airline tramway on Hollyburn Ridge. Council turned down this proposal because of ongoing negotiations with the provincial government—and then World War II exploded and all such large ambitious plans were put on hold.

The first rope tow on Hollyburn was in fact a small portable brought in by Ed Oakley around 1943. After the war, the number of tows built accelerated. Norm Deacon installed a tow on the Popfly across First Lake from Hollyburn Lodge in 1948.

Ed Oakley's portable rope tow, early 1940s. (JACK OWEN COLLECTION)

First Lake rope tow, ca. 1948. (PAUL JAFFARY COLLECTION)

At times children on the First Lake rope tow found themselves airborne, as shown in this March 1964 photo. (ALEX SWANSON COLLECTION)

Some say the name came from a description of a bumpy trail or ski run; another version is that it was named after "Pop" Burfield, although the use of the name predates his presence at Hollyburn. The Popfly tow was lucrative, and Fred Burfield thought that he should get a cut of the profits. Norm Deacon, on the other hand, thought the added coffee and refreshments business brought to the lodge by the ski lift business should satisfy Burfield. One night someone took a chainsaw to one of the rope tow towers and destroyed the tow. Norm Deacon backed off and Harry Burfield took over, installing another tow.

Norm Deacon soon returned to the tow-building business. In 1947 Bob McLellan, a professional mechanical engineer and designer of light suspended structures, designed a rope tow system for Deacon which transported skiers to the top of each of two slopes at West Lake, using a single drive system powered by a 110-horsepower motor

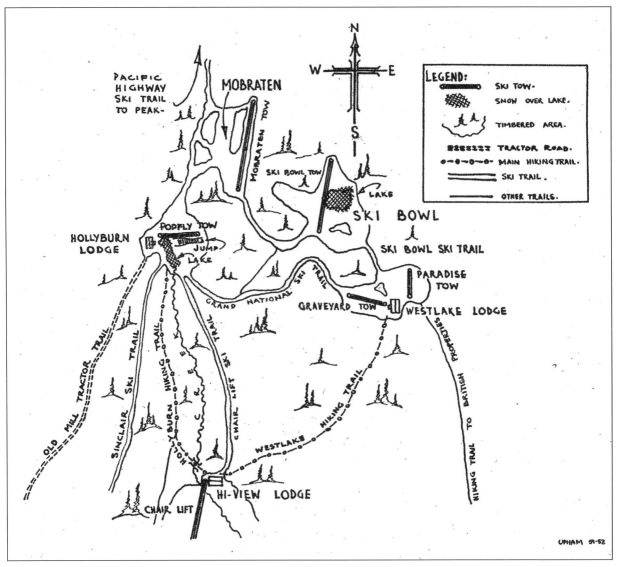

Ski tows and trails at Westlake/Hollyburn, ca. 1948.
(HANS AND MARGARET BRUNNER COLLECTION)

using seventeen car wheels as pulleys. At the same time, McLellan designed tows near Westlake Lodge named Graveyard and Paradise. In the fall of 1948, night skiing started on Saturdays on Paradise, the Westlake Lodge beginners' hill.

At one time, eight rope tows ferried skiers on Hollyburn: Suicide, Graveyard and Paradise at Westlake, a double tow at West Lake, a beginners' run at Hi-View, the Popfly at Hollyburn Lodge and a short-lived tow at Mobraaten, which was hampered by a creek at the bottom. In the 1960s Burfield added Blueberry at First Lake at right angles to the Popfly to create a beginners' hill. A remnant of the West Lake tow still

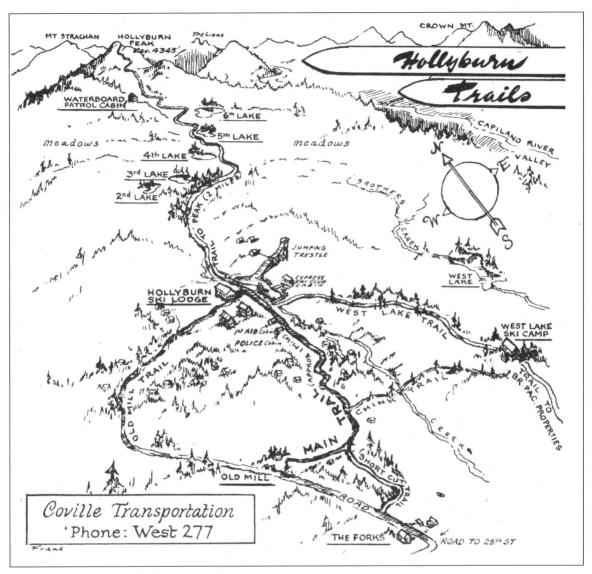

Routes to Hollyburn and major trails, late 1940s. (WEST VANCOUVER ARCHIVES. WEST VANCOUVER ARCHIVES COLLECTION. 108.WVA.DOC)

survived in 2008 on the north edge of the lake. Most of the rope tows were shut down by 1965 by inspectors because of safety concerns, although the Popfly operated until about 1983. This tow was hugely popular with elementary school children in the '50s and '60s. Young skiers were often lifted some distance above the snow, much to the delight of the youngsters, but to the concern of watching parents and tow operators.

After the Suicide rope tow was installed in 1954, the linked hills of Suicide, Graveyard and Hells Bells at Westlake became the venue for a popular club race for the local kamikazes, called the Deacon downhill—organized by Norm Deacon. The apocalyptic names have been explained as follows. Starting off at the top, skiers on Suicide would naturally end up in the Graveyard. The race course then continued past Westlake Lodge and down to the afterlife of Hells Bells. Skiers might also enjoy the blissful slopes of the beginners' hill—Paradise. Together, Suicide and Graveyard served the longest ski run serviced by rope tows in B.C. at this time.

In the 1940s, Jim Huff, owner of the service station at 25th Street and Marine Drive, started a truck service on the road built for the Heeps logging project. He generally went as far as the Forks store, and to the Old Mill site if possible, transporting about two hundred people on Sundays. While he was supposed to take only gear, as he did not have a license to carry passengers on the city streets, many passengers jumped aboard at the top of 26th Street as it entered the forest. These were not exactly luxury trips. Not having four-wheel-drive, this truck had trouble navigating the road if there was mud or snow. Jim Harman recalls that everyone had to jump off and push it around the corners.

In 1948 Hi Coville, a commercial fisherman looking for a way to make some money on the off-season, teamed up with Dick Lawrence, Thorne Schindler and Bill Theodore to start a service from Dundarave Café to the Forks store. Two war-surplus

The Forks store, 1940s. (ERIC CABLE COLLECTION)

Half-track with skiers at the Old Mill site, late 1940s.
(WEST VANCOUVER ARCHIVES. COLVILLE FAMILY FONDS. 003.WVA.COL)

half-tracks, complete with armour, transported skiers for seventy-five cents. These often caught fire, and when they began breaking down, Hi and his partner Bill Theodore replaced the tracks with wheels; he also added a four-wheel-drive war-surplus ambulance vehicle for further transportation. They carried as many as 50,000 people yearly, although many still hiked when the trucks were busy.

Despite these attempts to keep the Hollyburn spirit alive, interest declined. In his "Hollyburn Ridge: A Snapshot of its Historical Cabin Record," Karl Ricker notes, "From 1957 onward decay had set in; the old guard was 'pensioning' out, and the new cabin owners were too few to mobilize mountain enthusiasm." While in the early days it took a whole summer to cut enough wood to keep a cabin going for the winter, when chainsaws became common, all that work could be done in a few days. Paradoxically, the easier things got, the fewer people were interested. Bert Baker recalls it as ironic that more people came up to Hollyburn when there was no road than after the building of the Cypress Bowl Road—although, as will be seen, all that changed with the development of the Cypress downhill area.

CHAPTER 10

Chairway to the Stars

*Although the chairlift had many deficiencies, people of my
generation remember it with great fondness. Some might say they had
a love-hate relationship with the chairlift—its idiosyncrasies and
perceived dangers were part of its charm. I remember vividly the
occasions when I rode the chairlift after a fun-filled day of skiing—
Point Grey and the strait were lit up by the waning light of the setting
sun. As most rode alone, it was a time of peaceful reflection.*

—DON GRANT, HOLLYBURN HERITAGE SOCIETY

Grouse Mountain's first double chairlift opened in 1949 on the south slope of the mountain, extending from the end of Skyline Drive to Grouse Village, east of the present gondola. Road access up Mount Seymour in 1950 led to rapid expansion of this ski area and attracted many new visitors. Lifts were constructed at resorts in northwestern Washington at Mount Baker and Stevens Pass. Sun Valley, Idaho, which had developed in the 1930s, was another popular destination. Hollyburn was being left behind. A chairlift was needed if it was to continue being competitive. Hi Coville took up the challenge.

Like many who loved Hollyburn, Coville wanted to share its splendour. The company formed to build the lift, with Roy Sims as the president and Coville as the vice-president, purchased a 150-acre (65-hectare) strip of land for the lift from British Properties, and thirteen acres from other private owners. On January 17, 1951, the Hollyburn Aerial Tramway opened for business. The face of skiing at Hollyburn was redrawn. Dreams of competing with the finest ski resorts anywhere fuelled their efforts. Shortly after the chairlift started to operate, Coville completed Hi-View, a

Hi-View Lodge, ca. 1960. (CITY OF VANCOUVER ARCHIVES, HAROLD MERILEES FONDS, ADD.MSS 426, LOC. 561-C-1, FILE 3, W. CUNNINGHAM PHOTO—VANCOUVER DAILY PROVINCE)

$60,000 lodge at the lift's terminus, which gave skiers a feel of alpine luxury—certainly a far cry from roughing it in the old Hollyburn Ski Camp.

Built of steel and concrete, with eight towers, at a cost of $250,000, the lift took just twelve minutes to cover what was previously a hike of a couple of hours. It was designed and the material furnished by Riblet Tramway Company of Spokane, although 98 percent of the material was of Canadian manufacture. Founded in the 1890s in Nelson, the company had honed its skills by building lifts in the tropics to transport bananas.

Gregarious Oscar Pearson from the Hollyburn Ski Camp days, who had recently returned from Sweden, was hired to run the lift and greet people on their arrival at

The chairlift from the top loading platform, 1955.
(WEST VANCOUVER ARCHIVES. HOLLYBURN RIDGE COLLECTION. 148.WVA.HRC)

the top. He lived in a small cabin he had built behind Hi-View Lodge. Harry Burfield moved his ski shop from Hollyburn Lodge to the top of the chairlift. The lodge restaurant served turkey and steak dinners on the main floor and held weekly dances and occasional plays. Staff accommodation was upstairs. Entertainment included movie nights, with baseball on skis as one of the more exotic activities. Bill Theodore ran the HAT (Hollyburn Aerial Tramways) Inn at the bottom of the lift.

One of the casualties of this development was the Forks store, which Coville had bought from the Sambrooks in 1945. It was abandoned soon after the chairlift opened and, along with the Bread Lady's cabin and Snefty's Coffee Shop, demolished.

At 1,800 metres the Hollyburn single chairlift was at this time the second longest in North America. Park ranger Ted Russell suggests this may have been a disadvantage, as the gradual incline meant a longer cable and more towers and wheels to maintain, compared to that needed for a lift to service a shorter, steeper hill. Its 135 single seats could transport up to 300 passengers an hour from the lower terminus at HAT Inn at 300 metres (at the extension of upper 26th Street) to Hi-View Lodge at

▲ Oscar Pearson's cabin near the top
station of the Hollyburn chairlift, 1963.
(ALEX SWANSON COLLECTION)

◀ David Swanson arriving at the
top of the chairlift, August 1964.
Small children riding alone faced
a scary trip over the deep Marr
Creek canyon with the safety
bar at chin level.
(ALEX SWANSON COLLECTION)

850 metres (about the same elevation as Westlake Lodge). From here skiers still had to hike to First Lake and its rope tows, or do some more hiking and skiing up to the Hollyburn Plateau and Romstad's. Permission to extend the lift into West Vancouver land was refused, which made it less efficient than it might have been. Still, it was certainly a lot quicker and more convenient than hiking all the way, or even riding Coville's truck.

By the fall of 1951, lights had been added to some of the runs near Hi-View Lodge. In conjunction with the lights on Westlake's Paradise run, this created the most extensively lit ski area on the North Shore. In 1954 two sideways-facing double chairs and two baskets that could ferry down injured skiers in stretchers were added. Music also enhanced the good-times atmosphere.

Some, including Fred Burfield, thought that putting in a single chairlift was a mistake. For many of the very young or overly cautious, a ride alone on a lift suspended many feet above the ground was not something they wanted to repeat. The traverse over the deep chasm of Marr Creek could be especially daunting. In addition, the chairlift's capacity was insufficient when it came to transporting large crowds down the mountain on a Sunday afternoon, resulting in long lineups. No public bus served the starting point of the chairlift. Its description by some Hollyburners as a lift going from nowhere to nowhere may have been a little harsh, but in fact Hollyburn, except for the one chairlift run, was still relying on rope tows to serve the actual skiing areas. Grouse, in contrast, had built a chairlift on their big ski hill in 1953–54. Hollyburn followed suit in November 1955 when a run was cut that followed the top part of the chairlift, allowing skiers to navigate about a quarter of the chairlift route down to tower twenty-two, and reload there. But this was usable only in years when there was a heavy snowfall.

Don Grant recalls his childhood memories riding the chairlift with mixed emotions:

> I made my first trip up the chairlift at the age of seven. It was both thrilling and terrifying to be on the lift without a parent close at hand. The ride past each tower was quite bumpy and caused the chair to rock. Fortunately the ground beneath seemed quite close. By the time I reached the loading platform at the bottom of the ski cut, I was feeling a little more relaxed and confident. Then came the traverse over deep Marr Creek Canyon. I froze, afraid that the slightest movement on my part might result in a death plunge. Later, I was able to convince myself that I had passed this character-building test with equanimity. My next door neighbour Scott McRae also remembers his first (and only) trip on the Hollyburn chairlift. He was so traumatized by the experience that he has not been on a chairlift since. On the return trip, Scott and his mother hiked to the bottom.

On the morning of June 6, 1965, Hi-View Lodge and the top station
of the chairlift were a smoldering ruin. Oscar Pearson's cabin on
the left escaped unscathed. (ALEX SWANSON COLLECTION)

Frequent breakdowns and stories of stranded skiers created major problems.
Miles Staley tells of his less than happy chairlift ride on December 24, 1951 or 1952:

> By early Sunday evening, heading for home, we lit our "bugs" and skied to the chair
> at 7 p.m. The chair lift was not in operation. My dad eventually found Oscar at his
> cabin and explained we needed to descend. Our packs were put in the "basket" and
> I (10 years old) was first on the lift. We were about 6 chair lengths apart, Dad at
> approximately tower 25-26 and I was at tower 19-20 when the lift stopped. We sat
> for 30 minutes or more, all the while Dad yelled and yelled for help. Feeling fright-
> ened and cold I felt the chair lift begin to slowly move backwards! We eventually
> made it to the top, got off and headed for the lodge-welcoming warmth and an ex-
> planation. Apparently there was no attendant at the bottom to assist. We waited an
> hour for the assistant to arrive. We got back on the lift thinking all was well. As we
> descended to tower 2, Dad noticed our packs on the way back up the lift. There was
> not an attendant at the bottom of the lift after all. We both got off the lift, leaving
> our packs to their upward merry way and headed home for Christmas Eve. Both my
> Mum (Peggy Staley) and sister Trudy were happy to see us home.

A fourteen-year-old boy later broke his arm when he fell six metres trying to get
off the lift by jumping on to the sixteenth tower. On another occasion Alex Swanson's
son David was being taken down on a toboggan but the lift operator, whom Alex
thinks was drunk, forgot to take off the handles. The handles hit one tower and a fall
of thirty feet to the ground below was only narrowly averted.

The most serious breakdown came on the night of December 26, 1962, when fifty-six young people were trapped on the lift for up to three hours when four youths swinging chairs at the bottom flipped the chairlift cable out of the pulley. The sagging cable pulled a chair into the crossbeams of a lift tower, pulling it down. Police and firemen used twelve-metre aluminum ladders and ropes to rescue passengers stranded up to sixty metres off the ground. While no one was seriously hurt, this was hardly good public relations.

By the mid-1960s, poor weather, breakdowns and vandalism contributed to dulling the lift's competitive edge. When Hi-View Lodge burned down in 1965, the lift had already fallen into disuse, and the contents of the Lodge had been packed down the mountain. Construction at Whistler had already begun, with its network of gondolas and chairlifts ushering in a new world of skiing possibilities on the West Coast.

The Hi-View fire started at the top loading landing. Gasoline had been poured there, and it is believed that someone purposely set the fire, which quickly spread to the lodge. Remnants of some of the concrete footings and a few towers remain, and the odd chair might be found in the bush. In the past forty years nature has done its work in reclaiming the area, although the cut was still, in 2008, visible from Point Grey in Vancouver.

For the next decade after the lift burned down, few except cabin owners visited Hollyburn, although access from 15th Street to the old Heaps logging road made getting to the lodge by four-wheel-drive possible in summer. As Rick Crosby says, "Once the chairlift burned, it was like turning a valve off."

CHAPTER 11

Cypress:
Visions and Revisions

There has been great havoc here,
An enormous slaughtering.
Some David has run amok
With a relentless sling
Leaving a broken green silence,
An apocalypse of wood
And a new void in the universe
Where Goliaths once stood.

—PETER TROWER'S "GOLIATH COUNTRY"

The bowl formed by Black Mountain and Mount Strachan provides a magnificent setting for a ski/recreation/park area, which was not lost on early skiers and others. In the prescient words of journalist Stewart McNeill, it was "like being in the middle of the biggest Olympic stadium you could ever imagine."

Former ranger Jack Wood states that when he came out of the service in 1945, he and Eric MacIntosh looked into the possibility of developing Cypress Bowl, but soon realized the project was beyond their scope. The Vancouver Ski Club was the first to weigh in with serious plans. In 1948 the Vancouver Ski Club approached the provincial government with a request for redeveloping Cypress Bowl for downhill skiing, but the government of the day showed no interest. Again, in 1960, Jack Rockandel, then president of the Vancouver Ski Club, wrote the provincial government suggesting that "the Government grant the Vancouver Ski Club a lease to develop Cypress Bowl. We propose to finance the development by the sale of interest-bearing bonds or debentures." Plans were "to make Cypress the greatest Ski and Park area in B.C."

View over Cypress Bowl to Georgia Strait from Hollyburn Peak, ca. 1950.
(JACK ROOCROFT COLLECTION)

In February 1960, West Vancouver parks commissioner R.F. Spray agreed to seek approval for the development of the bowl as a ski area; in March, West Vancouver councillors were impressed with a helicopter tour of the area. But without sufficient capital the plan did not advance.

In 1963 the West Vancouver Parks Planning Reconnaissance Report by G.A. Wood notes that making Cypress Bowl a park while continuing to allow private enterprise would make little sense, as the goals of the investors in recouping their investment would likely conflict with sound park planning. "It is strongly recommended that, if private development is permitted to proceed, this should not be mixed with public park status." But the provincial government was unwilling to commit the necessary capital for a ski area, and West Vancouver did not have it. The alternative was a private company, and (hopefully) sufficient controls to keep the company honest.

In the early 1960s Earl Pletsch, a jumper on the 1948 Canadian Olympic ski team in spite of having lost an arm in a railroad accident, was manager of the Mount Seymour ski operations, and president of Vancouver's Alpine Outdoor Recreation. On June 2, 1964, he and his friend Chuck Eadie formally submitted a $10 million proposal for a four-season commercial/recreation development on Cypress. The grandiose plans included a fifty-passenger gondola to the top of Black Mountain, two chairlifts up Mount Strachan, a man-made lake, a trout farm, a hotel-motel-restaurant complex and parking for 3,000 cars. Facilities for curling, tennis, golf, skating, riding stables, trap and skeet ranges, an archery range—even a non-denominational church—were proposed. The writers of the proposal waxed eloquent: "Well-planned, well-administered outdoor recreational areas adjacent to large centres of population arouse the interest of the imprisoned city-dweller in new activities." Up to 700,000 visitors a year were envisioned. Reeve Alex Forst and his West Vancouver council, seduced by the idea of having a world-class resort in their backyard, were strongly supportive.

Unforeseen at this time was the way this mega-project would collide with the cultural transformations of the 1960s. The pro-development Social Credit government and West Vancouver municipal council became enmeshed in a battle with those who found this project an ideal focus for their anger against an establishment that was perceived to put profits before human and environmental values.

From 1964 on, a young and aggressive MLA (later B.C. premier) from Coquitlam, Dave Barrett, spearheaded opposition to this project, urging that it be suspended, and the 1944 intent to set aside this area as a park be respected. On the other side, recreation minister Kenneth Kiernan and his provincial government colleagues joined the West Vancouver representatives in giving the ski development their wholehearted support. The 1944 plan to dedicate the land to a park was, in Kiernan's view, "not even worth the paper it was written on." Technically he was right, although it is clear that the original intent of the 1944 plan was that this area would become a park.

When the Hollyburn chairlift burned in 1965, the need for more efficient ski access to this area became more pressing, and no doubt many wanted to believe that the proposed development was within desirable parameters. On August 19, 1965, West Vancouver released a community plan, and two days later the provincial cabinet approved a bylaw governing development of the area. The next year cabinet passed two orders-in-council, one reserving 3,700 acres (1,596 hectares) for recreational use, and one reserving 1,700 acres (650 hectares) in which development would take place. The "village core" would occupy about twenty-two acres (nine hectares) in the valley.

Pletsch's Alpine Outdoor Recreation contracted with T.E. (Teddie) Osborne, president of Mountain Timbers Limited, to clear land for commercial establishments and ski runs. Logging began on a sixty-acre (twenty-four hectare) site, which early plans designate as a parking lot. But the development of the actual ski infrastructure was glacial. By January 1968, West Vancouver reeve Alex Forst was becoming nervous about the logging of non-designated areas which should not be logged, and the lack of any construction at all. By July 1968, 10 million feet of lumber had been clear-cut on Cypress Bowl with nary a bag of cement in sight, and Mountain Timbers showed no sign of slowing down. Alpine's own report in June 1966 had indicated that only a little over 4 million feet would need to be cleared.

According to Ken Farquharson, forest ranger Jack Wood deserves credit for being the first to blow the whistle. He sent seventeen memos to the municipal manager and council members, twelve in 1968 alone, plus many photographs, calling for a stop to the logging. Like most who opposed what was going on, he was not against development, but wanted it done the right way. But there was no response. Slash from the logging was not in fact cleared up until years later, at a cost to the taxpayer of a half million dollars.

In November 1968, the Varsity Outdoor Club organized a trip by five outdoor clubs (but no ski clubs) to view the effects of this logging. Farquharson, spokesperson for the Save Cypress Bowl Committee, stated they were "aghast" at the destruction. He raised hell at what he saw as out-of-control logging in Cypress Bowl. Alpine's Chuck Eadie countered that the logging was being carried out at a loss, as much of the timber was of inferior quality, with the balsam infected by woolly aphids. Most of the timber was indeed low grade balsam and hemlock, but some excellent yellow cedar was also trucked out for lucrative sale on world markets. Even lands and forests minister Williston claimed that there was "nothing wrong with what is happening here," and both the B.C. Forest Service and the Municipality signed off on the logging of the area. Councillor Don Lanskail was dismissive of objections, but Farquharson states that Lanskail's perception was coloured by his friendship with Chuck Eadie.

West Vancouver's municipal council hired C.D. Schultz and Company Limited to prepare a report on logging operations (although this firm had previously acted as consultants for Alpine's original proposal). This report, which dealt only with the financial aspect of the logging, concluded that this phase of the operations had been carried out at a loss—although Dave Barrett later stated that a $468,000 profit had been confirmed by B.C.'s chief forester L.E. Swannell. It does raise the question of why anyone would engage in logging if it was not at least perceived to be profitable. Finally the excessive logging and absence of ski infrastructure became impossible to ignore. West Vancouver Mayor Forst finally urged Minister Williston to stop the charade, which he did on November 18, 1968.

Strapped for cash, and perhaps feeling their options were closing off, Eadie turned to the deep pockets of the Benguet group of companies. On November 5, 1969, Benguet purchased a 75 percent interest in Alpine for $1.5 million and created a new company, Valley Royal Development Company Limited. Having a northern resort in this area would be a great tie-in for their cruises up the west coast. Benguet had recently merged with the Grand Bahama Port Authority, which derived 10 percent of its revenue from gambling casinos and was alleged to have mafia connections.

Farquharson states that he became aware through someone in the civil service that the Crown had leased 732 acres (256 hectares) of land to Alpine on the top of Black Mountain and in Cypress Bowl without going through due process. These leases had

Cypress Bowl from Hollyburn Peak, showing the extensive clear-cuts, April 1969.
(ALEX SWANSON COLLECTION)

then been transferred to Benguet. He phoned outspoken talk-show host Jack Webster, who blew the case wide open. Benguet appears to have believed, based on what they were told by Alpine Outdoor Recreation, that their purchase entitled them to proceed with residential subdivisions.

Seven hundred citizens who attended a raucous three-and-a-half hour council meeting on November 24, 1969, voiced their displeasure. They called for an immediate halt to the Cypress Bowl project, with Ken Farquharson arguing that Alpine Resources was interested only in real estate speculation. Acting West Vancouver mayor Art Langley and his council immediately requested the provincial government to order cessation of all operations pending a judicial review. On November 27, the *Vancouver Sun* reported that the provincial government had bowed to public pressure, cancelling the leases and refusing to allow development of Cypress Bowl to proceed as long as Benguet controlled the developing company.

These leases covered 300 acres (122 hectares) at the top of Black Mountain, an area around Yew Lake and an area at the north end of the bowl. Benguet, their development plans shot down, wanted $1.2 million compensation from the provincial government, or permission to go ahead with residential land sales, without which they did not believe ski development would be economically viable. Their plan was to subdivide 700 acres into 2,000 lots at $6,000 each for healthy revenue of $12 million that would then (supposedly) be used to finance the development of the ski area. The provincial government rejected this plan.

Williston gave Alpine until May 31, 1970, to come up with development plans that did not include Benguet, but their efforts to secure financial backing elsewhere were unsuccessful. Mountain Timbers, who had been clearing the land, went bankrupt, leading the Bank of Montreal to seize the felled timber in Cypress Bowl. Ken Farquharson states that the only reason they could declare bankruptcy was that they had transferred all their money to Panama.

Without sufficient funding, the private developers opted out. But a strong demand for skiing and recreation still existed. On January 27, 1971, Williston reported that the government would proceed with public money. A paved road into Cypress Bowl was completed in 1973 at a cost of $8 million. Further preparation by West Vancouver Council in March 1972 included trading 587 acres of its land on Hollyburn Ridge for 593 acres (239 hectares) of land around Eagle Lake, which supplied water for residents from Cypress Creek west to Horseshoe Bay. No overnight accommodation and no commercial operations, other than the ski rental and ski school, would be allowed. As plans developed, downhill skiing was cut back, while other recreational activities such as cross-country skiing, tobogganing and hiking received greater emphasis.

Dave Barrett, NDP premier from 1972 to 1975, continued his unrelenting environmental advocacy. The protection of Cypress was for him a key issue in saving an important part of our environmental heritage. He states that his vocal support of park

The Cypress Bowl highway, showing some of the clear-cut areas above
Hi-View Lookout, May 1976. A hang glider can be made out in the centre.
(ALEX SWANSON COLLECTION)

status even alienated some in his own party. In 1975, shortly before their electoral defeat, Barrett's government designated the area a Class A category 6 park, meaning that it was a park with two or more purposes: in this case recreation and preservation of the environment. The May 1976 Cypress Park Master Plan provides an eloquent vision of its functions:

> The facilities that will be developed and the management procedures that will be utilized will encourage diverse recreational uses of the Park by many segments of the public and will encourage family use of the entire area. This diversity of opportunity ranging from downhill skiing to nature contemplation will be tempered by the inherent qualities of the landscape and the provision of existing and proposed park opportunities elsewhere in the Lower Mainland region.

The 2,104 hectare area was bordered on the west by Howe Sound, on the north and east by the ridgetops of Mount Strachan and Hollyburn Mountain and on the south by West Vancouver. In 1982 the addition of the Deeks Lake area, linked to the existing Cypress Park by the Howe Sound Crest Trail, brought the total area of the park to 5,269 hectares The downhill ski area opened in January 1976, with chairlifts up Black Mountain and Mount Strachan, a rope tow on the bunny hill on Mount Strachan, and ancillary services. Total cost for the downhill area, including the building of facilities, runs, trails and purchase of snow-clearing/grooming equipment was estimated at between $4.5 and 5 million.

When the Social Credit party returned to power in late 1975, they brought their free enterprise philosophy to the table. The ski area over the next years certainly did not live up to expectations as a commercial venture, if that indeed should be the benchmark. On July 7, 1983, parks minister Anthony Brummet issued a press release stating that Cypress Bowl would be leased to the private sector, with the area remaining crown land. Meanwhile, Wayne Booth was becoming a part of the picture. He had operated a ski school at Seymour for the past five years, and in 1982 the provincial government granted him permission to operate a ski rental concession in Cypress Provincial Park.

The government, having recently purchased the cross-country operations from the Burfields, packaged it for sale with the downhill area in 1984. The successful bidder was Wayne Booth and his partner Brett Hughes and their company Cypress Bowl Recreations Limited (CBRL). The price was $500,000, plus 2 percent of revenues received. This was similar to the deal worked out with the Seymour ski area, which also received a fifty-year lease. Wayne Booth states that there was little information

Chairlifts on Black Mountain and Mount Strachan, March 1976.
(ALEX SWANSON COLLECTION)

available on which to base his purchase. The previous management did not pay hydro bills (as it was a government operation), had no record of food services, no skier visitor statistics and no record of the cost of snow removal. Even at a good price, the purchase was a risk.

No transfer of land occurred and park status was not cancelled, but neither did public consultation take place. The book value of the facilities was about ten times the lease price, although at the same time Booth had to operate within the parameters of a public park, which placed far greater restraints on development than if it had been private property.

Wayne Booth brought a great deal of energy and efficient management practices to the operation. He increased the estimated 20–30,000 downhill skier visitors of 1983–84 to 85,000 the next year, and eventually to 300,000. (There are now about 500,000.) His initial plan emphasized the development of night skiing, and then improvement of the existing runs, as this is what attracts skiers. As Booth says, the money is in lift tickets, not hot dogs. Plans for improved base facilities were postponed until the new master plan was accepted, and for now he made do with a series of trailers with some modest additions.

Booth is a controversial figure. He is generally admired for his thorough understanding of the ski industry; he developed Cypress from a skiing backwater to a highly successful and well-balanced resort. Many consider him to have a genuine feeling for the people involved at Cypress. He has been generous to local groups such as the Hollyburn Heritage Society, sponsoring a New Year's party at Hollyburn lodge and turning over the $1,400 profit to them. He also sponsored groups such as the Varsity Outdoor Club and the Pioneer Skiers' annual reunions. He started revegetation work on the logged area on the south side of Strachan, and a 1992 report suggests he had plans to plant trees.

But Booth could also be a difficult person, especially for those with environmental concerns, with his aggressive push to expand the Cypress ski development into pristine areas. He felt that this was necessary for its financial viability, but his abrasive, often confrontational, management style made his tenure at the helm a rocky one.

In the winter of 1984–85 CBRL subjected use of the cross-country trails, which under BC Parks had been free (they were ungroomed and untracked), to a charge as compensation for grooming them. People who were accessing the back-country area via ungroomed trails now were also stopped. While most skiers accepted the right of CBRL to charge for the use of groomed trails, fees for the use of ungroomed trails generated strenuous opposition from the back-country skiers and their supporters, who argued that the Parks Act says the public has unrestricted access to the parks. A letter from Parks Minister Anthony Brummet to the Federation of Mountain Clubs April 18, 1985, stated that "it was the intent to embody within the permit a guarantee of the rights of park visitors to the 'unimproved' sections of the Hollyburn Nordic area free-of-charge." An article in the October 7, 1964, *Vancouver Sun* had stated that the West Vancouver Council supports the ski development as long as "the public is guaranteed absolute freedom of access to the summit of Black and Strachan."

CBRL argued that anyone on the ungroomed trails could say they were heading to the back-country and thus avoid paying the regular cross-country fees. In addition, sanitation, rescue and parking facilities could be used without charge. The conflict intensified over the winter, with some skiers saying that CBRL staff photographed them without their permission, physically blocked their paths and swore at them. The Save Cypress Bowl Committee was reactivated and the conflict came to a head with a ski-in protest on March 1, 1986, by a group of fifty angry skiers. The leader, lawyer John Beltz, was arrested for skiing in the permit area without a ski pass by a police officer slipping and sliding, and looking somewhat foolish high up on the ski slopes. Legal action against Beltz and the Save Cypress Bowl Committee chair Lynn von Krosigk was eventually dropped, although some committee members such as Katharine Steig feel it would have been better if it had gone to court and the issues been resolved at this time.

In April 1986 an agreement was reached between the government and CBRL to allow skiers a public corridor for free access to the wilderness areas, but only on Hollyburn. Many felt that this corridor was too narrow and steep to allow for safe descent on cross-country skis. A "gentleman's agreement" provided for access through the downhill area to the Howe Sound Crest Trail, but the Federation of Mountain Clubs expressed concern that the route up the northwest side of Strachan was also too dangerous.

The Cypress Bowl protest in the cross-country parking lot, March 1986.
(STEVE GRANT PHOTO, COURTESY FRIENDS OF CYPRESS PROVINCIAL PARK)

Booth continued to push for expansion of downhill skiing. After considerable negotiation with the government, a revised permit issued on November 5, 1986, expanded the controlled recreation area to include the south peak of Mount Strachan in the alpine ski area and the land above the power lines in the Nordic ski area toward Hollyburn Mountain. At the same time the sensitive ecological area of Yew Lake was removed from the permit area. Sky Chair, a lift purchased from Apex Alpine Resort in 1990, provided access to the top of Strachan. Two slashes on Strachan left over from earlier logging made for good ski runs, and the altitude and vertical drop gave Cypress more intermediate terrain, which was one of the features that Booth felt the ski area needed for success. Booth also had his eye on a snow bowl on Strachan above the existing Sunrise Chair which could be serviced by a gondola. This would make for an ideal beginners' area, especially in bad snow years. A restaurant on the top of Strachan could provide food services. Or so he planned.

In spite of the changes on the hill, the renovated trailers used for services were

The Cypress Bowl protest, March 1986. West Vancouver police question
John Beltz while Wayne Booth (in glasses) looks on.
(STEVE GRANT PHOTO, COURTESY FRIENDS OF CYPRESS PROVINCIAL PARK)

woefully inadequate. Grouse was moving ahead with some highly sophisticated and
diverse development. And Whistler was becoming the epitome of resort chic. Booth
pushed for a master plan that included commercial expansion expected to cost $30 to
40 million. New lifts on Black and Strachan, downhill runs on Hollyburn, a restaurant at the top of Mount Strachan, expanded parking, and an "Independence Lodge"
intended for the promotion of recreational opportunities for the physically challenged
were on the table for discussion. Facilities would also be provided for skating, concerts,
festivals, banquets and conferences. Booth argued that he needed expanded facilities
and an expanded permit area to remain competitive. The only way expanded facilities
could be financed, he argued, was by more skier visits, which in turn created the need
for more facilities.

To oppose this expansion, John Beltz formed the Friends of Cypress Provincial
Park Society in January 1990. This society, which has continued to be active, works
to promote the preservation of the natural environment and to promote the park's
special historical and cultural features, and to foster through education and understanding an appreciation of the park's natural features. The society aims to "ensure
that the wilderness areas of the park are not any further encroached upon or reduced

in size by private, commercial development, or for that matter public development, inconsistent with the preservation of the wilderness nature of the park."

The late big tree hunter Randy Stoltmann, the coordinator of the B.C. big tree program, submitted a report in April 1990 to the Ministry of Parks on big trees in Cypress Park. He argued that the presence of some of the oldest recorded trees in British Columbia made for excellent research and educational opportunities; he urged park management to protect these cultural and natural heritage resources. Cypress Park contained significant amounts of old growth. Some of the large diameter yellow cedars at risk were well over 1,000 years old.

Although BC Parks refused to authorize Cypress to take its master plan to the public, Booth was not intimidated. On April 10, 1992, CBRL presented its Master Concept Plan in West Vancouver's Park Royal South Shopping Centre. The two development options he presented were "No Expansion," indicating what was feasible if the permit area was not extended. The second, titled "Adding 100 Hectares to the Permit Area," focused on the expansion of the downhill ski area on to Hollyburn Mountain. Hollyburn provided a location for some much-needed intermediate runs, but it also had an extensive stand of 100-plus hectares of old growth.

BC Parks presented a different view of the planning process on June 27, 1992, with their three options. Option X represented no expansion of the permit area; Option Y, partial expansion on Black Mountain; Option Z, the full expansion plan on to Black and Hollyburn Mountains. Even with its three options, BC Parks became increasingly unwilling to co-operate with CBRL, while the latter, perceiving that Parks was siding with environmentalists, launched a lawsuit.

In May 1995 Brian Williams was appointed Chair of the Cypress Park Special Planning Commission to try to reach a mediated settlement. His seventy-seven recommendations were accepted in full by cabinet in September 1995 and formed the basis for the new Cypress Park Master Plan. This denied expansion outside the ski company's existing permit area, including Hollyburn Mountain and the south slope of Black Mountain. However, proposed expansion within the permit area would allow fifty-three acres (twenty-one hectares) of old growth to be cut, including trees over 1,000 years old. A small hundred-seat restaurant on top of Mount Strachan was recommended. The master plan was signed on June 25, 1997. While most considered this an acceptable compromise, Friends of Cypress Provincial Park Society co-chair Katharine Steig was less impressed, stating that the park's master plan would negatively affect the park's natural environment and recreational opportunities. The playing field would change substantially when Booth sold the operations.

In the meantime, Milan Illich, who had become Wayne Booth's partner in 1991, was becoming reluctant to commit the major time and money necessary for the development that the plan needed. Initially, Booth was prepared to go it alone, but when he started to have some health problems, he reconsidered. He was by now in his mid-fifties, and thought that perhaps involving himself in a $45 million expansion project at this time was being too aggressive. Time to step back. In February 2001, Booth sold the ski operation to Boyne U.S.A. resorts. Founded by Everett Kircher and owned by his son John, Boyne U.S.A. owned five other ski resorts in the United States. The complete management staff of CBRL was kept on, with Linda Swain becoming manager, and her husband Bobby Swain project manager.

That summer Kircher replaced Black Mountain's Eagle Chair with the area's first high-speed quad. He also replaced what must have been one of the last rope tows anywhere with a slow quad, the Easy Rider. In June 2002 their revised master plan, much to the surprise and satisfaction of the environmentalists, incorporated most of the changes for which the environmentalists had fought so vigorously over the years. Kircher wanted to end the controversy that had plagued Cypress for decades; he also wanted to position himself to land some of the 2010 Olympic events. His manager, Linda Swain, who had acquired a thorough knowledge of the operations during her twenty years with Cypress, became the only female manager of a ski area in Western Canada. Her approach has also emphasized consultation and collaboration with the various stakeholders.

The contentious plans for building a restaurant on top of Strachan were abandoned, as were plans for a gondola lift, which involved cutting trails through old growth on the southwestern slopes of Strachan. Also shelved were plans for a series of tubing chutes through old growth on Hollyburn Ridge, a chairlift above the Howe Sound Crest Trail, a lift near the Collins run and Frank Lake and a Jetstream ski run into former out-of-bounds areas.

Instead, they focused their attention on developing the area of Black Mountain that had been logged in the late '60s. An additional quad chair and nine new runs provided the upper intermediate and advanced runs that balanced their terrain. Generally the new owners displayed sensitivity to the new rules of environmental stewardship. They were also successful at attracting 2010 Winter Olympic events.

In late 2005, Boyne Resorts sold their Cypress holdings to CNL Income Properties for $47,500,000 U.S., who leased them back to Boyne, who will continue operations under a twenty-year lease with four five-year renewal options. CNL (which changed its name in March 2008 to CNL Lifestyle Properties) is based in Orlando, Florida, and is an investment trust focusing on leisure and lifestyle properties in North America. Cypress's assets are owned by CNL, which funds capital development, while Boyne manages and funds operations. This enhances Boyne's access to capital, which is particularly important for the development of the 2010 Olympics. Cypress now attracts well over a million people annually—40 percent in the winter and 60 percent in the summer. This is the highest day use of any provincial park in British Columbia, although many of the summer visitors do not get past the Hi-View Lookout.

CHAPTER 12

Skiing under Control: Safety and Instruction

✦

*There is plenty of reason to give the idea of
controlled racing thought. . . . It might be the answer to
our need for a saner goal for perfection in skiing.*

—*HIKER AND SKIER*, JANUARY 7, 1937

In the early days, the ski clubs took care of their own injured warriors. A cavalier, often macho attitude prevailed, with the odd fractured ankle considered an acceptable price to pay for the pleasures of the downhill rush. As mentioned earlier, there was even one fatality, when in January 1938 Ben Harstad fell from the top of the First Lake ski jump and landed on his head. But gradually a more common sense approach developed. The first ski patrol on Hollyburn was started about 1930, with Bert Brink's old cabin near Sixth Lake becoming the first aid shack. Bert was instrumental in organizing the first group of skiers on Hollyburn to aid and assist those who had met with mishaps. "Ski guards" started in about 1938, and the Canadian Ski Patrol system was formed January 1, 1940.

Along with the need for safety, ski instruction developed as a matter of course. While in the early years instruction was at best haphazard, depending on the time and goodwill of the more accomplished skiers, it soon became clear that a need for more regular instruction existed. On January 30, 1935, the Cavell Ski School was started under the auspices of the Western Canadian Amateur Ski Association (WCASA) at

▲ Hans Brunner instructs a group of skiers on
Hollyburn Ridge, 1950s. (ERIC CABLE PHOTO,
HANS AND MARGARET BRUNNER COLLECTION)

◀ Title page to Hans Brunner's "Austrian Ski
School" early 1950s. Booklet used by ski classes
on Hollyburn Ridge. (HANS AND MARGARET
BRUNNER COLLECTION)

Gus Johnson teaching a group of skiers near Hollyburn Ski Lodge, 1958.
(BURFIELD FAMILY COLLECTION)

West Lake. In early January 1936, Jack Croup of Hollyburn Pacific Ski Club was hired as the first certified ski instructor in the West, and ski instruction was started by the Vancouver Ski Club on January 12. The West Vancouver Council was responsive to ski club requests for grants, which were used partly to defray the cost of lessons to members and to improve club facilities.

In 1936 the Provincial Department of Recreation and Physical Education appointed Finn Fladmark (Hollyburn) and Ned Stevens (Grouse) as ski instructors. The earlier method of strapping on the boards and going like hell was gradually replaced by a greater emphasis on technique and safety. "Skiing under control" became the new mantra; the kamikazes of the early years were to some extent replaced by

Hollyburn ranger Ted Russell checks on Donna Swanson after a skiing accident on the Popfly hill, April 1964. The Hollyburn rangers were well trained in first aid, and also organized search parties for lost skiers and hikers.
(ALEX SWANSON COLLECTION)

students well-schooled in the snowplow and proper ways to fall. Sitzmarks, the impressions made in the snow by a fall, were to be filled in.

The new chairlift that opened in 1951 greatly increased the potential market. Fred and Evy Burfield started free ski lessons in the First Lake area in 1951, and in December of that year Austrian Hans Brunner was hired to lead the immensely popular free ski school sponsored jointly by the *Vancouver Daily Province* and Hollyburn Aerial Trams. Taught by up to twenty-eight instructors, these classes not only introduced a whole generation of the young and not-so-young to skiing, but brought an Austrian rigour and discipline to the sport that often contrasted with the freewheeling Scandinavian exuberance of the earlier years. In 1953, the year that Hardy Rowley became the chief instructor, these classes drew 500 students. Meanwhile the *Sun* ran an equally successful ski school on Grouse. Each of the mountaineering clubs also sponsored a course of instruction in mountain safety first aid. Iola Knight recalls Phyllis Munday's instruction on how to make a stretcher using tree branches and ski poles, and how to cure snow blindness with used tea bags.

In 1949 a newspaper article noted that the St. John Ambulance maintained a Forest Aid Ski Patrol through the No. 84 West Vancouver Nursing Division. After a boy became lost on Grouse and died of exposure in 1951 a 125-person Mountain Emergency Squad was formed, chaired by Sam Taylor and composed of representatives from skiing and mountaineering groups such as the BC Mountaineering Club.

In 1965 the North Shore Search and Rescue Organization (NSSR) was founded, growing out of a request in North Vancouver for volunteers for civil defence on the North Shore in the eventuality that the Russians dropped a nuclear warhead in the vicinity. The organization has developed into one of the largest and most respected wilderness rescue organizations anywhere. The mushrooming popularity of skiing and other outdoor activities beginning in the '60s inevitably led to more people venturing where they should not, and calls to North Shore Search and Rescue went from seven to ten annual calls in the early years to 111 in 2005. Much of their work aims at preventing accidents before they happen, to inform people of the need to prepare for wilderness conditions so as to avoid situations such as occurred on April 28, 2005. On this date two backpackers were retrieved from an area north of Cypress Bowl as they were trekking to the Lions. They had no crampons, ice axes or snowshoes, and one was wearing running shoes. The organization has established escape trails on the North Shore mountains to help lost snowboarders, skiers and hikers find their way off the mountain. And at the end of every day that the Grouse Grind is open, someone from NSSR conducts a sweep of the trail.

In a 2004 interview, Gerry Brewer, who has been involved with this organization from the beginning, recalls how they developed their skills through an eclectic gathering of varying techniques. Joel Harden of the U.S. border patrol started a training program on human tracking, and the Canadian military taught them spotting from aircraft. A helicopter flight rescue system is used extensively, often avoiding the aggravation of injuries that can result by packing the injured over rough terrain in a stretcher. Women have been a part of the team since about 1970; as of 2004 a total of forty-two active members were on call. Each member is committed to his/her activity and connection with the outdoors: "the kind of person that whether it is summer or winter, night or day, good weather or bad they are comfortable being out there."

Peggy Pratt rests after an accident while descending Strachan gully on the west side of Mount Strachan in the early 1940s. Her brother Herb Woods is on the right. The hiking party was heading for the Lions when Peggy slipped on the loose shale and cut her leg badly. The hikers formed a stretcher party and carried her several kilometres down Mount Strachan and Hollyburn Mountain. (JACK AND PEGGY PRATT COLLECTION)

Brewer describes the basic structure of their approach, which includes careful strategic planning for all eventualities:

That's why we have the gazelles and the plodders. The gazelles are the people who can just go like hell—give them a first aid pack, a map and say call's there, get there, stabilize the guy, when you find him, give us a call let us know what we have to bring in in equipment. And then the luggers come in with the load of equipment needed to do the job. We normally work on the basis that we'll do it on the ground. At the same time, we recognize that we can also overfly it and do it by air. But if you lose your machine, lose your weather, lose your light, then you've already mobilized and set yourself up to do it the hard way. . . . You become acutely aware of the fact that you've got to think all the time about what it is that I'm doing, what alternatives do I have, what's the best one and how do I cover it off if that isn't working?

Public education and videos have become a major part of their outreach. With his brother Dave, Gerry Brewer wrote a booklet—how to manage a search and rescue operation—that has been circulated internationally. He has developed a week-long course now offered by the Justice Institute. The most precise and detailed maps of the North Shore in existence have been developed to give rescuers exact information about the terrain. In addition, the North Shore Search and Rescue teams often manage or assist in rescues in other jurisdictions in both Canada and the U.S.

And rescue work is more than just going out and tramping through the bush. While some calls are simply to find lost skiers and hikers, investigating crime and suicide scenes is also a part of their work. Brewer describes some of the psychology involved in one actual case of a missing person search: ". . . people do all kinds of things, including park cars in parking lots up the mountain and then disappear across the border with their playmate. And you check the insurance bureau and there's a couple of policies, and he figures, well, the policy will pay the wife, I'm out of here, my conscience is clear. And the guy's picked up in Vegas about three months later."

North Shore Search and Rescue is a volunteer organization that levies no charges for its services; they do not want people refusing to report accidents or missing persons for fear of being charged. It is a highly professional organization which has become a model for other jurisdictions as to how the job should be done. Each year a number of people owe their lives to its efficient and well-planned searches.

CHAPTER 13

Golf Courses, Mountain Bikes and Old Growth

With an adult on a bicycle,
there's hope for civilization.

—H.G. WELLS

Over the years many groups have cast interested eyes on the area west and south of the old Nasmyth Mill site at the last switchback on the Cypress Bowl Road—one of the areas closest to West Vancouver that remains accessible and undeveloped. Much of it was logged by Heeps in the 1940s, but then it was forgotten for some years. Forgotten, that is, until some golf course developers became intrigued with the possibilities of fairways sliced through this spectacular terrain.

Plans for a golf course on Hollyburn Ridge date back even earlier, to a time when 1931 zoning bylaw 478 provided for a golf course here. Dormant for a generation, the plans resurfaced in 1969 with a proposal that Benguet be given land for a golf course to get them out of Cypress Bowl. The proposal was rejected. By this time West Vancouver municipality had accumulated 350 acres (142 hectares) for a golf course, much of it from the old Heeps logging operations. What makes the proposal for a golf course especially contentious is that in some of the upper areas the forest is old growth. Nevertheless, considerable revenue heading the District's way was expected to result from any completed project.

With the building of the new Cypress Bowl highway in the early '70s, plans progressed. West Vancouver mayor Art Langley was an enthusiastic supporter of the new golf course, and landscape architect J.W. Neil was commissioned to prepare a preliminary analysis. His 1973 report for the municipality of West Vancouver waxes lyrical about the possibilities:

> Topographically, the area appears to be ideal for the development of a most interesting golf course. It is a commanding site, offering vistas overlooking Burrard Inlet and the City of Vancouver. The terrain, mostly gently sloping, is sufficiently variable to make the course challenging to the golf course architect and subsequently to the players.

Yet the 1976 Hollyburn Ridge Committee was not moved by such lyricism, and recommended against the golf course. Mayor Donald Lanskail chaired the committee, and although he was himself a member of the Capilano Golf and Country Club, went along with the majority.

Even with Hollyburn Ridge Committee's negative recommendation, plans for a golf course continued. A proposal to study the viability of a golf course appeared in the 1978 Parks and Recreation Plan. Two years later, in their 1980 Official Community Plan, West Vancouver once again proposed a golf course as a possible use for the area. These plans revived in 1987 when West Vancouver officials invited course proposals, selecting Cypress Bowl Recreations Limited to develop a private golf course and country club. In December of that year, Ancore Development did a feasibility study on developing 350 acres (142 hectares) of land for this purpose, and a proposal appeared again in the 1988 Official Community Plan. A 1989 report by Talisman Land Resource Consultants suggested that a 27-hole course was feasible if "rigorous environmental protection standards are incorporated into the final design and maintained throughout the implementation process." It was well known that opportunities for golf on the North Shore were limited, and it was becoming an increasingly popular sport among West Vancouver's aging population.

Plans now moved rapidly, although opposition grew along with support. In July 1990 the West Vancouver District Council signed an agreement with Cypress Ridge Golf Company Limited to develop a golf course. Meanwhile, in May 1990 a group of West Vancouver residents formed the Friends of Cypress Ridge, aimed at protecting the old growth area from golf course development. This group, it should be noted, was distinct from and not connected with the Friends of Cypress Provincial Park, which had been formed in January 1990. Paul Hundal of Friends of Cypress Ridge filed a B.C. Supreme Court petition to overturn the golf course rezoning bylaws. At a May council meeting 200 residents packed the council chambers expressing their vocal opposition to the destruction of a portion of old growth forest. The consultants'

THE VOICE OF NORTH AND WEST VANCOUVER

north shore news

SUNDAY

Beating
family violence

Lifestyles: 25

November 18, 1990   Classifieds 986-6222   Office, Editorial 985-2131   Display Advertising 980-0511   Distribution 986-1337   56 pages   25¢

Golf course protest

NEWS photo Terry Peters

CANDLES, SIGNS and plenty of youthful energy enlivened the north end of the Lions Gate Bridge Friday morning as protesters urged commuters to reject golf course development at Cypress Ridge.

Protesters at the Lions Gate Bridge urge rejection of the golf course.
The *North Shore News*, November 18, 1990.
(NORTH SHORE NEWS)

arguments that a golf course would enhance the wildlife and environment did not impress these residents.

Nevertheless, in September 1990 Mayor Donald Lanskail and his West Vancouver Council voted to petition the provincial government to transfer the restrictive covenant that prevented development of the golf course. This covenant restricted lease time to twenty years and required property to be used recreationally. A golf course, in the province's view, was commercial, not recreational. Paul Hundal, the founder of Friends of Cypress Ridge, responded by filing a petition with B.C.'s Supreme Court arguing council improperly adjourned the public hearings on the golf course rezoning application.

Friends of Cypress celebrate victory for the "Cypress Ridge" Old Growth, November 1990.
(IAN ROWLES PHOTO, COURTESY FRIENDS OF CYPRESS PROVINCIAL PARK)

The opposition, termed by some "a small element of tree huggers," mustered a sustained campaign. Katharine Steig states that those against the golf course were in fact a much broader coalition of people concerned with the environment, including well-known citizens such as Jim Graham, Paul Hundal, Tony Tobin and Will Pollock. Friends of Cypress Ridge provided the main organizing focus. Many young students came out in force, and some feel that their demonstrations at Lions Gate Bridge were crucial in turning the tide against the golf course. A broad segment of West Vancouver's population objected to development above the 365-metre level, and the golf course project was seen as opening the door to residential and other development farther up the mountain. Michael Feller, a UBC forest ecologist, examined the proposed golf course area and reported that a number of fairways would be cut through old growth forest.

Katharine Steig states that there was little understanding of the importance of old growth at this time; Randy Stoltman and others were instrumental in raising the level of public consciousness about the unique and irreplaceable nature of old growth. Mounting public pressure forced the municipal government to hold a referendum on November 17, 1990. The choice was simple—accept or reject the construction of a golf course. If accepted, the choice was between a twenty-seven-hole golf course with a minimum 50 percent of public playing time and the retention of twenty-two acres (nine hectares) of old growth forest, or an eighteen-hole course with 30 percent public playing time and the retention of all old growth forest. Apparently Lanskail thought the golf course side would win, but an expensive brochure in support of the project, paid for by taxpayers and distributed to all West Vancouver residences, backfired. Apparently the so-called tree huggers were more numerous than expected. The golf course proposal was voted down.

Plans for the golf course were now history, but the use of the land remained to be determined. West Vancouver mayor Mark Sager formed the Municipal Mountain Lands Committee, which largely took over the role of the Friends of Cypress Ridge. This committee recommended that these lands be put up for protection through referendum. In November 1993 the people of West Vancouver voted to have this fifty-four-hectare area at an elevation of between 510 and 770 metres set aside. A thirty-hectare stand of old growth in the northern area contains trees that regenerated after a major fire in the early 1600s, the only near-pristine old growth in West Vancouver at this elevation. Some trees are 900 years old. Bridging the coastal western hemlock and the mountain hemlock zones, this area has considerable diversity of vegetative life. The absence of introduced species enhances its ecological integrity.

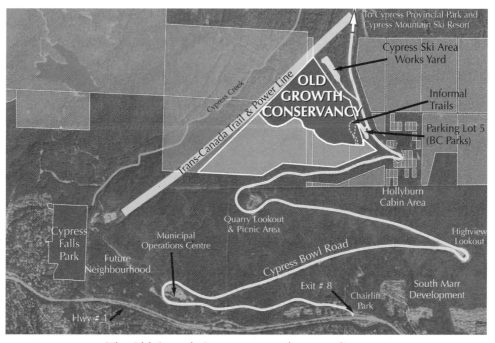

The Old Growth Conservancy and surrounding area.
The proposed mountain bike park is the light grey area south of the conservancy.

The park was, however, little used, and mostly slipped outside of the area of public interest over the next few years. In June 2006 Council approved a name change to Old Growth Conservancy as a result of the District of West Vancouver Strategy for Protection Management Plan, suggesting that it was less a place for public recreation than a place for the preservation of an ecologically significant area.

Mountain biking was the next potential trial that the area was to face. By the early 1980s this sport had made its way up from Marin County in California to the challenging terrain of the Canadian West Coast, bringing with it a whole new way of exploring the wilderness. Most of the early riders were responsible and environmentally conscious, but others were freewheeling cowboys with an attitude, who often cut down trees for trails and caused extensive erosion with their aggressive riding. This led to resentment from hikers and other users.

Many early bikers soon found existing trails insufficiently challenging; they pushed themselves and their bikes to new limits on purpose-built trails. Ross Kirkwood is generally credited with building the first trail on the North Shore in 1983: the Kirkford, on Grouse. Todd "Digger" Fiander began his work in 1986, extending trail design to new limits of his fertile imagination. His videos have had a worldwide impact. More recently he has been hired by the Cypress Bowl Ski Area to build trails for the Black Mountain Bike Park.

The North Shore's steep and rugged slopes provide some of the best biking terrain anywhere. As riders became more skilled, trail designs increased in difficulty, which in turn made riders more skilled. Then bike design began to play a part, with full suspension and disc brakes releasing some outrageously free spirits. Creative ramps, ladder bridges, linked teeter-totters and big launches earned this area a reputation as one of the most radical mountain biking venues anywhere, with many features of the creative trail designs reappearing throughout the mountain-biking world. Log rides are becoming skinnier and higher, and riders have done drops of thirty-five feet (ski jumping, anyone?). As one younger rider says, "If you can ride the North Shore stuff, you can ride anything." With their camaraderie and the adoption of their sport as a way of life, mountain bikers are in many ways reincarnations of the skiers of a half-century earlier. Energetic self-reliance and a passionate devotion to exploring the limits of their sport drive both.

In the winter of 1997, over a few beers in Lynn Valley's Black Bear pub, Todd Fiander, Mitch Diem and Lee Lau initiated the North Shore Mountain Bike Association (NSMBA). Charges for use of the trails on Fromme Mountain were rumoured, and there were fears that housing developments would take away trails on Cypress,

A mountain biker takes to the air at the Cypress Bike Park on Black Mountain, July 2005.
(JOFFREY KOEMAN PHOTO, COURTESY CYPRESS MOUNTAIN)

Grouse and Seymour. Many recognized that there would be benefits to all if they could clean up a public image that a few of the less responsible riders had sullied. They organized their first trail maintenance day in 1998. These events became practical ways to teach trail etiquette and open up dialogue between riders and the public. By 2005 the NSMBA had 1,100 members.

Mountain biking's credibility was also enhanced when athletes like Alison Sydor and Lesley Tomlinson, who often trained on the North Shore, began winning big international races. Wade Simmons, Ryan Leach, Thomas Vanderham, Richie Sley and Micayla Gatto are a few of the other respected names in the North Shore biking community. The World Mountain Bike Festival was held on the North Shore from May 21 to June 5, 2005. This event brought in substantial cash to the community— as any pub owner would agree.

Mountain biking has changed considerably from the early days when it was a way of exploring some of B.C.'s many wilderness roads and trails. Some of the more traditional riders continue this type of riding in the Brothers Creek area, but mountain biking in the past few years is now mostly a downhill activity, with the heavy bikes and the technically demanding trails generally not suited for uphill pedalling. This has made for more wear and tear on the trails, since bikers can cover many downhill kilometres in a day, especially with a van to take them back up to the top. While bikers are now generally much more sensitive to their impact, the increased number in a relatively small area puts more stress on the environment.

In West Vancouver, the prime terrain for biking is a mixture of private and municipal land, which has complicated the use of this area. West Vancouver was home to some of the best trails on the North Shore such as the Reaper and the Pre-Reaper, but nearly all of them are at least partly on private land, mostly belonging to British Pacific Properties (BPP). In 1999 after a young rider fell and was badly injured while riding on one of these trails, the municipality, concerned with liability, took chainsaws to the elaborately constructed trails and destroyed many of them. British Pacific Properties followed suit on their own land—liability and environmental damage were the main concerns. Some hikers were also upset at the usurpation of their trails, as hiking and the more technical mountain bike structures are incompatible.

The municipality's aggressive action initially put them at war with the mountain biking community, but in 2000 a Mountain Bike Task Force, formed from a broad spectrum of community groups, including West Vancouver municipal representatives, British Pacific Properties and the mountain biking community, led to a less confrontational and more co-operative atmosphere. The committee agreed that the only structures that would be allowed on West Vancouver mountain bike trails would be ones similar to those found on hiking trails—no stunt structures. The majority of the maintenance would be undertaken by the District of West Vancouver, with assistance from the North Shore Mountain Bike Association "if they so wished."

British Pacific Properties' official position is that trails on their land are not permitted because of liability issues—they do not carry liability insurance. In practice BPP does not monitor trail use closely, and Andrew Pottinger of BPP states that in recent years there has been very little friction. BPP also recognizes that since they signpost only the public accesses to their land, it is quite possible that mountain bikers could venture on to their land and even build trails without realizing they were on private land.

In August 2004 a feasibility study by the municipality recognized that the increasing number of competitive and recreational bikers in West Vancouver needed a place to ride, and that the Cypress area was the most suitable. School teams from West Vancouver have been extremely successful in competition, but have no place to train in West Vancouver. The report argues that "A formally recognized mountain bike park could showcase West Vancouver's ability to promote sustainable mountain biking, while assisting in meeting the recreational demands of community members and visitors." A park was proposed for the land immediately south of the Old Growth Park, but at two kilometres by 0.6 kilometres it would not have a whole lot of room. As there is no natural vegetation buffer between the proposed biking area and the Old Growth Conservancy, many are concerned that bikers would, knowingly or otherwise, venture out of their designated area.

Many West Vancouver municipal administrators are now favourably disposed toward mountain biking. But navigating the devious routes of municipal politics is proving more difficult than the narrowest mountain bike ladder bridge. Plans for a bike park have been put on hold. The 2006 "Parks and Open Space Background Document" states that "Efforts are underway, in consultation with a variety of trail users, including the North Shore Mountain Bike Association, to properly plan for and manage mountain biking in the municipality."

Even British Pacific Properties now recognizes that mountain biking is here to stay, that it has progressed from an activity for those on the extreme fringes to a respectable sport engaged in by people of all ages and social strata (including many who call the British Pacific Properties home). While they still reserve the right to dismantle structures that appear on their private land, they are now coming to see the financial advantages to the community of this activity, as mountain bikers are generally an affluent lot with an average annual salary, according to a 2004 report, of over $75,000. The economic impact on the North Shore was in 2005 an estimated $30 million.

If the present mountain-biking trails cannot be accommodated, they may be moved. That being said, today's trail building tends to use sustainable methods and natural structures. The iconoclastic rebels of twenty years ago are now mostly somebody's parents, and often established members of the community. Many issues remain to be worked out in West Vancouver, but people are talking, and problems are at least being ventilated. There is still, however, no overall plan for the North Shore that would lead to effective marketing of one of the top mountain biking areas in the world. Not much in the way of maps or trail signage. No doubt that will come.

CHAPTER 14

Swifter, Higher, Stronger (and Greener): The Olympics at Cypress

✦

Cypress Bowl is like being in the middle of the biggest Olympic stadium you could ever imagine.

—STEWART MCNEILL, JOURNALIST

In 1928 Rudolph Verne enthusiastically promoted Hollyburn as having all the attractions of St. Moritz, Switzerland, the site of the 1928 Olympics. Nothing came of Verne's early enthusiasm, but then in the 1960s politicians and media began to turn to the Whistler area as a possible Olympic venue. Proposals were submitted for the Vancouver/Whistler area for the 1976 and 1980 Winter Olympic Games, with former Hollyburn jumper Henry Sotvedt in charge of the ski jumping plans for the 1980 games. The BC Department of Recreation and Conservation prepared a feasibility study in 1974 (before the Cypress downhill area opened) which was optimistic about the physical capability of Cypress Bowl to support the snow events in the 1980 games.

Although insufficient vertical existed for a men's downhill race, the 1974 report stated it would be possible to establish a downhill course on Cypress that would meet International Ski Federation standards for women. Giant slalom and slalom could be easily accommodated. A 70/90 metre jump could be built on the north face of Black Mountain, with the Nordic events in the Hollyburn area. Facilities for bobsleigh and luge events could also, so the report stated, be accommodated on a single course on

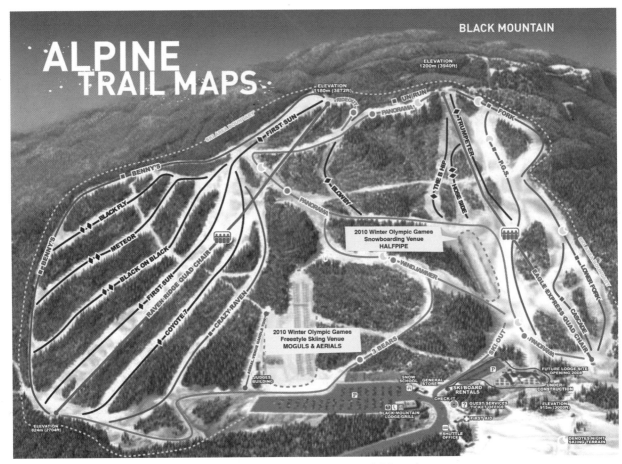

Black Mountain, showing new runs and Olympic venues.
(MAP COURTESY CYPRESS MOUNTAIN)

Hollyburn Mountain. Holding the closing ceremonies at the ski jump site was also considered, although the report concluded that "the positive effect of speeding up the rate of park development is negated by the nature of development that would occur."

With hindsight it was fortunate these plans did not materialize, as they would certainly have destroyed much of Cypress Bowl's environmental integrity. But over eighty years after Verne's visionary dreams, some of them are about to become reality. In the 2010 Winter Olympics, Cypress Bowl Ski Recreations will host the six freestyle skiing events of men's and women's aerials, moguls, ski cross and six snowboard events: men's and women's parallel giant slalom, halfpipe and snowboard cross. Ski cross and snowboard cross are new events, in which four competitors go head to head in a race in which position, not time is the deciding factor. Freestyle and snowboarding events are among the most popular spectator sports of the games and, for a short time, the eyes of the world will be on Cypress.

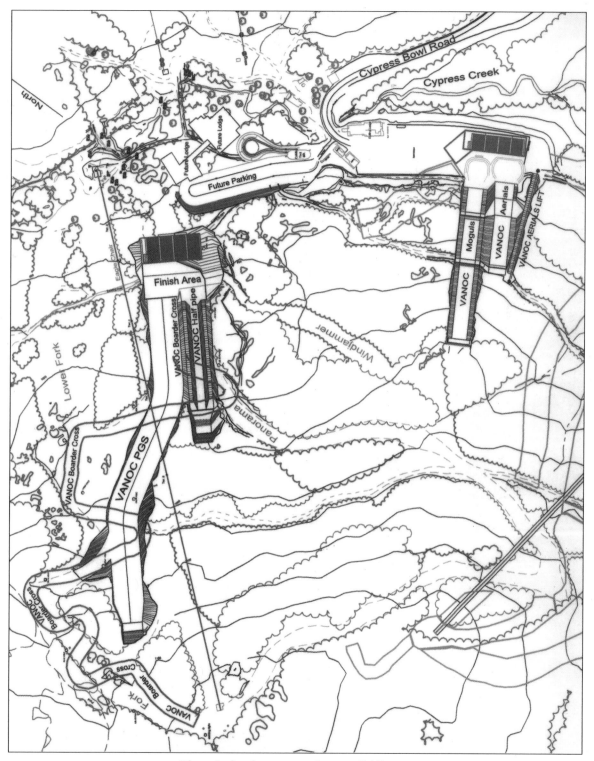

Olympic development at Cypress Ski Resort.
(MAP COURTESY CYPRESS MOUNTAIN)

Aerial competitions at the World Cup, Black Mountain, February 7, 2008.
(JOFFREY KOEMAN PHOTO, COURTESY CYPRESS MOUNTAIN)

The games, awarded to Vancouver/Whistler in July 2003, will be held February 12–28, 2010, with the Paralympics shortly after on March 12–21, although Cypress will host no Paralympic events. As the Olympics approach, the planning phase is intensifying. High-level test events in all the sports are being held in the two years leading up to the Olympics. A World Cup event was held at Cypress in February 2008, and in February 2009 the Vancouver Olympic Committee (VANOC) will put on another World Cup event at Cypress in which they will be testing their systems. VANOC will be testing thirty-five issues such as accreditation, security and traffic to make sure that the actual Olympic events run glitch-free.

Cypress's current construction manager Bobby Swain states that the original

An aerial jump at the Mogul Competition at the
World Cup, Black Mountain, February 9, 2008.
(JOFFREY KOEMAN PHOTO, COURTESY CYPRESS MOUNTAIN)

request for events went to the Olympic Bid Committee in about 1998. At that time it
went nowhere, but when it became evident that Whistler was overloaded, Cypress
became a logical backup. About 12,000 people a day will visit Cypress during the
Olympics, but in fact that is no more than a busy weekend day at present. No new
roads will be needed, and water and sewer can be accommodated by existing structures (sewer is now linked to the West Vancouver system). Regular ski operations will
be suspended during Olympic competition because of security concerns, and frequent
shuttle buses should take the pressure off parking. At any rate, private cars will not
be allowed access. For some years now, the owners of Cypress have been busy renam-
ing the combined ski area as "Cypress Mountain," a name that seems to be catching
on with at least some of the skiers and journalists writing about the area, and that is
the name being used in Olympic promotions.

The Olympic events will be held on new venues that have been developed on
Black Mountain. Fourteen million dollars from the provincial and federal govern-
ments is helping fund infrastructure, which will include a long overdue day lodge

Snowboard cross, Black Mountain, March 5, 2008.
(JOFFREY KOEMAN PHOTO, COURTESY CYPRESS MOUNTAIN)

scheduled to open in time for the 2008–09 ski season. The new lodge will include a restaurant, rental shop, ski school facilities, ticket office and a place to hold corporate events. Nine new high-level intermediate and expert ski runs, the first in twenty years, have been added to Black Mountain on a brand new forty hectare area, increasing the skiable area by 40 percent. These will be accessed by the newly named Raven Ridge Quad Chair, which is the 1997 Sunrise Quad Chair moved over from Mount Strachan. The new name comes from a bizarre activity that some local ravens have adopted of removing rubber from windshield wiper blades and door seals from cars in the nearby lot. The new lift on Strachan is the high speed Lions Express quad chair.

In the nearby cross-country area, a new facility—including food and beverage services, rental and a ticket office—will eventually be built near the current buildings in the cross-country area. The current buildings will then be torn down, with their functions moved into the new cross-country facility. This phase will not be completed until after the Olympics.

In the downhill area, snowboarding, halfpipe and snowboard cross will be accessed by the existing Eagle Express quad chair, while lift access to freestyle will be by the new handle lift beside the venue. Freestyle sites are located above the existing parking area and in close proximity to snowboarding. The mogul course will be 275 metres long and forty metres wide, with a twenty-seven degree slope, and have a per-

Half-pipe competition at the Canadian Nationals, Black Mountain, April 4, 2008.
(JOFFREY KOEMAN PHOTO, COURTESY CYPRESS MOUNTAIN)

manent starting hut. The halfpipe, using the Panorama run, will be 4.5 to 4.7 metres high, with a slope of sixteen to seventeen degrees. The venues will be a great legacy for the development of youth programs. Already some talented youngsters, such as Vancouver's Keira Leung, are making their presence felt. Colin Boyd, president of the Cypress Ski Club, is looking forward to the infrastructure that will make mounting events easier. For example, hard wired cables will be in place for timing, which will make obsolete the current practice of running cables over the snow for each event.

The snowboard Parallel Giant Slalom will have a running length of 550 metres and an average slope of eighteen degrees, using the existing runs of Trumpeter, Gully and Fork. The new sport of snowboard cross will use an upgraded Fork run. Each of the two venues will have spectator capacity during the Olympics of 12,000, made up of 8,000 temporary seats and 4,000 standing. With the seating dismantled after the Olympics, the sites will be capable of hosting the Canadian series, North American and International Ski Federation World Cup competitions in freestyle and snowboarding.

In the unlikely event of mild temperatures, manager Linda Swain says snow cats will transport snow from higher up the mountain. Also included are snow-making facilities (an Olympic requirement) that were developed in the summer of 2007. The original plans to use Cypress Creek as a source for water for snow-making were scrubbed because of environmental concerns. The next proposal was for a snow-making reservoir in an old gravel pit north of the Montizambert Creek domestic pump house, but here again it was felt that the impact on the environment would be too great. Finally the reservoir was designated for a sawmill site near the old Sunrise Quad chair. While this is closer to the ski operations, it has meant transplanting the common butterwort and the three-leaved goldthread, the rarest plants in the park, to a different area for their preservation. The various stakeholders generally agree that this is the best solution.

The relocation of the historic Baden-Powell trail to the north side of the Black Mountain ski area has proved one of the more contentious issues. The upgrading of the border cross run has pushed the rerouted Baden-Powell trail to a route just beyond the edge of the ski area. It is rough, steep in one place, and much of the trail is sur-faced with gravel. Linda Swain says this trail is a work in progress; further develop-ment will include benches and perhaps stairs in some of the steep sections.

Original Olympic plans have been modified considerably through consultation with the various stakeholders to minimize environmental damage while providing facilities that meet or exceed international standards. The initial proposal to cut seven to twenty-two old growth trees in the area of the freestyle facility has been modified, and no trees older than forty years were cut for any of the venues. The new develop-ment has created a sense of excitement and anticipation that pervades Cypress as the resort is transformed. Few would want to trade the new high speed quad chairs and designer coffee for a two-hour slog up hill and root beer made from the water in First Lake. And yet . . . while progress is inevitable, the pioneers can remind us that this is not without a price, and human values must remain primary. As the sign above the entrance to Hollyburn Lodge still says:

| Be of good cheer | If sad and alone | Here you will find |
| You're quite welcome here | Let this be your home | A welcome most kind |

CHAPTER 15

Into the Next Millennium

✦

Hollyburn is worth preserving because of its beauty
and because of what it provides to the human spirit.

—JIM CRAIG, OUTDOORSMAN AND RETIRED LAWYER

Hollyburn tests our humanity. Can a large population learn to be a good steward of its environment when there are so many tempting advantages, at least in the short term, to being a bad steward? Can a large consumption-driven population curb its appetite for a once pristine wilderness in its backyard? Not many would say we deserve an A in these subjects, but neither have we failed the test. We stumble blindly on, not seeing as clearly as we should, but moving ahead with glimpses of the trail, hoping our vision enables us to navigate the next bend.

The struggles caused by an interface between a large urban population and a more-or-less wilderness area continue, and no doubt will create further problems and issues that future citizens will need to resolve. But while Hollyburn has taken more than a few knocks in the past, it is an affirmation of the resilience of nature that much of the quiet beauty of the Hollyburn/Cypress area survives. Peace and solitude are still available only a few feet from any of the mountain parking lots, but continual vigilance will be needed to ensure Hollyburn's continued role as a refuge from urban pressures and a treasure house of nature's diversity.

Meanwhile, politicians, environmentalists and others strive to effect a balance in dealing with the often mundane issues that affect the nature of this area. On March 11, 2002, West Vancouver City Council voted to close the West Lake road, the Hollyburn Ridge cabin area access road and the Grand National Trail to commercial dog walking. Illegal tree-cutting is potentially a more serious problem. In May 2003, a thirty-metre-tall yellow cedar three metres in circumference and about five hundred years old was taken out illegally. Possible ways of dealing with tree-cutting and similar problems include satellite surveillance, cameras mounted on towers, and acoustic recognizers programmed to detect specific sounds. None of these possibilities has yet been acted on, but ways to discourage tree rustling will need to be found.

In recent years environmental reclamation has come increasingly to the foreground. Assessment of resources has led to a wider recognition of the importance of local streams. North Shore Streamkeepers have engaged in a number of projects, including restoring habitat, planting stream banks, surveying streams and increasing public awareness. Concerted efforts have been undertaken to make many of them again hospitable to salmon and other fish, which once played such a central part in the lives of First Nations people who lived on the inlet.

The Cypress Creek enhancement group under the North Shore Streamkeepers received $10,000 in 1997 for a fish habitat assessment on lower Cypress Creek. Marr Creek has also received a great deal of attention in the face of setbacks, such as floods in 1955, which were caused by natural forces aggravated by deforestation and upstream housing construction. Tailed frogs and long-toed salamander frequent this watershed. A rare coastal-tailed frog has been observed behind the current day lodge, and northwestern salamanders around Yew Lake.

But where will Hollyburn go from here? I asked a number of people with different perspectives what they thought the area would be like twenty years from now, in 2028, and received thoughtful written responses from six. These were Katharine Steig of the Friends of Cypress, Catherine Rockandel of the Hollyburn Ridge Association, Alan Bardsley of the North Shore Mountain Bike Association and Don Grant, Iola Knight and Gordon Knight of the Hollyburn Heritage Society.

A general feeling exists that it is time to move beyond confrontation that often clouded past issues and into a more co-operative phase. Most saw development as dynamic—not all problems will have been resolved in twenty years, but a feeling of optimism pervades. Not surprisingly, a common thread in most of these responses is a desire to see the restoration of Hollyburn Lodge, which will celebrate its centennial in 2027. The restoration of the lodge is seen as a cornerstone of future progress, a test

Katharine Steig in the Old Growth Park, 1993.
(KATHARINE STEIG COLLECTION)

of the sincerity and seriousness of those with the resources. Don Grant and Iola Knight see displays of ski gear and photographs creating a tribute to the past in a ski museum as part of the lodge. Gordon Knight sees the lodge being heated geothermally from water in First Lake, with electricity mostly from solar panels. Plans are in progress to reconstruct the original Hollyburn Ski Camp, complete with cabins and a ski jump trestle.

Twenty years in the future Iola Knight imagines that "everybody comes up in a 'jet car'—a tiny vehicle that accommodates two and runs on a small very sensitive solar panel for energy to transport them up the Cypress Bowl Road." Knight also imagines

Catherine Rockandel during a Hollyburn Ridge Association cabin walkabout hosted by three cabin owners, December 2003. Catherine is holding a Christmas cookie. (DON GRANT COLLECTION)

that equipment will likewise become less intrusive and facilitate easier access to the trails. "[T]oday's skis are about four feet long, lightweight material with hard edges." Snowshoes have also become lighter, and she imagines snowshoeing debuting as an Olympic sport at the 2022 Olympics in Fairbanks, Alaska. Canadians will do well because of their training on the powerline hills around "Cypress Mountain."

Katharine Steig is pleased at the progress that has been made, but sees that work still remains for the next generation. She notes that the 1995 Cypress Park Special Planning Commission recommended an increased BC Parks presence in the park. This has not happened. As a result "trail conditions have deteriorated, and park maps, interpretive brochures and related park services are no longer provided by government." She looks forward to a time when BC Parks staff and others "work co-operatively to protect the park's natural environment and to provide appropriate recreational opportunities." Twenty years from now should find that "the park's natural diversity is protected and alien invasive species are kept under control. Hiking trails should be well maintained and damaged landscapes replanted." This will make it the

Iola Knight reading a poem by "Snefty" at the Pioneer Skiers' Reunion at Hollyburn Lodge, September 2000. (GORDON AND IOLA KNIGHT COLLECTION)

"exemplary park" envisioned in 1995. Steig hopes that "the old growth forest stands on Hollyburn, including West Vancouver's Old Growth Conservancy, remain intact, and that development is kept at the 1200-foot elevation."

Catherine Rockandel of the Hollyburn Ridge Association and her family have been closely connected to Hollyburn for several generations. "I have spent my childhood and adult life enjoying the simple tasks of chopping wood, carrying water and maintaining a cabin on Hollyburn. The quiet introspection of this time and the values of community I learned have defined my life." She hopes that over the next twenty years "the District of West Vancouver continues to recognize the Hollyburn community not just as a source of revenue, but as a community that supports the education, appreciation and stewardship of the natural and built environment." She looks forward to continued reinvigoration of the Hollyburn Ridge Association. "The fun-filled activities and events build relationships between cabin owners, ensuring that the social capital that is an integral aspect of the Hollyburn cabin community's history continues to flourish."

Alan Bardsley, a member of the North Shore Mountain Bike Association, sees that mountain biking, centred as it is on the lower slopes of Hollyburn, will experience a greater urban presence adjacent to their activity, but one that can remain complementary to and respectful of the environment. As envisioned in the British Pacific Properties' Rodgers Creek Area Development Plan, he sees an eco-friendly Cypress Village, located at the first switchback of the highway, as the staging area for mountain biking activity, with a coffee shop and pub providing a venue for pre- and post-biking socializing. (One might recall the importance of the lodges, the Forks store, and other commercial ventures in creating the early spirit of Hollyburn.) Trail days will be co-operative ventures between West Vancouver Parks and the North Shore Mountain Bike Association, with "English ivy, scotch broom and other invasive species . . . bagged and taken away for destruction." In spite of the growth of the adjacent urban community, he reminds us that "once you start down a trail, you are still enveloped in the lush green growth and can inhale the rich earthy aromas that connect you with the woods. The stress and worries of the outside world dissolve as you focus solely on the next ten metres of trail, safe in the knowledge that the value mountain biking brings to the area is recognized and appreciated."

Don Grant imagines a day at Hollyburn twenty years from now. He looks for-

Art "Snefty" Senft (left) and Gordon Knight at the Pioneer Skiers' Reunion, Hollyburn Lodge, September 2006. (GORDON AND IOLA KNIGHT COLLECTION)

Don Grant presents over 5,000 digital photos from the Hollyburn Heritage Society to Volker Schuster of the West Vancouver Archives, August 2006. Veronica Marshall (left) and Carol Howie (right) look on. (DON GRANT COLLECTION)

ward to enjoying a slice of freshly baked blueberry pie at the lodge (as the Burfields once made it) and the continuation of the cabin owners' annual fall festival. The Old Growth Conservancy will endure, with plans to create more protected areas within Cypress Provincial Park. Trails will be well maintained, with wooden walkways protecting the marshy habitat from human degradation. The Howe Sound Crest Trail will have been improved, "and will be recognized as one of the world's great ridge walks." The legacy of the 2010 Olympics will continue at Cypress, with "the upcoming World Cup aerials and moguls competition that will be held at the freestyle skiing venue on Black Mountain." Finally, at Hollyburn Lodge, "guests [will] enjoy a sumptuous dinner, and later in the evening they will be able to dance to lively traditional music played by a trio from Canada's east coast."

Hollyburn remains a place where all can find a healing renewal from the battles of urban life. The sibilant hiss of skis through a fresh fall of snow or the crunch of hiking boots on one of the many trails brings with it a profound peace. Hollyburn, nature's gift to us all, provides an imaginative capital that can, if invested wisely, be drawn on endlessly.

The Jeldness Tea Party

Early skiing in B.C. attracted, and perhaps helped to create, some outrageously free spirits who approached skiing with a boundless exuberance. Many of the early skiers from Hollyburn and elsewhere brought a *joie de vivre* to their sport and a willingness to test the limits that is today best embodied in extreme skiing and the more exotic forms of mountain biking. This spirit is nowhere better exemplified than by the legendary—if ironically named—Jeldness Tea Party.

Olaus Jeldness and a few friends started holding annual ski races in Rossland in 1896 when the Rossland Winter Carnival began. The original downhill race started at the top of Red Mountain and finished 2,000 feet (610 metres) below at the Allan House bar in Rossland. The last of these races appears to have been held January 27, 1899, with seven competitors. Jeldness won in a time of three minutes five seconds. The following account is a mythic recreation of these races, a Norse saga rooted in Canadian soil. It appears in *Hiker and Skier*, January 27, 1939, under the name of champion skier Nels Nelsen. A slightly different version first appeared in *The Rossland Miner* and was republished in Sam Wormington's book, *The Ski Race*:

On the occasion of the sale of a mine for which he received $75,000, [Olaus] Jeldness said unto himself; "I have made my wealth in these mountains and on the tops of the same, and now I will show how the ancient Vikings in my country extended their hospitality. I shall invite all my friends, skiers and otherwise to a combined feast and downhill race." There he cooked the various salt fishes of his native Norway and there was champagne in quantity to wash down the salty taste. To encourage the more faint hearted in the arduous climb, helpers were stationed at every turn in the trail with real Canadian refreshments. It was said one could stick his hand into any snowbank and pull out a bottle. Dr. Bowes and his ambulance had been stationed at the bottom of Red Mountain to carry away the dead and wounded. After the 25 or 30 guests had been dined and thoroughly wined Olaus got them group-started on the more than two-mile race from the top of Red Mountain to the Allan House bar, and then indeed was the harvest reaped. With shouts that would have put to shame an attack of Zulu warriors, the outfit started down the mountain. Trees and bushes trembled under the impact of down rushing bodies, skis were pointed and going in every direction if not altogether lost. Concussions and broken bones were numerous. Among the casualties were Ross Thompson whose legs, arms and head were badly cut from the out-cropping rocks; his skis were totally lost. Lionel Weber broke three ribs and his left knee cap. Jim Sword landed on the railway tracks, where he broke his nose and one ski. Frank Lascelles had one of his legs broken in three places and lost his voice. Joe Deschamps boasted of losing only one pound of white meat and of saving one of his skis. Archie Mackenzie, whose body jarred loose the first showing of pay ore in the Monte Cristo mine, was another casualty. In fact every guest in that famous downhill banquet of Jeldness was done to a turn with the exception of Olaus who ran the entire distance in one minute and fifty seconds, arriving at the Allan House bar boasting of having had a grand time.

While such races as the Jeldness Tea Party create our mythic history, similar skiing skills survive in today's world in different forms. Present-day aerial skiing combines jumping with aerobatics. Mogul skiing has its roots in the earlier days of skiing a century or more ago, when skiers jumped to clear rocks and other obstacles. Both these events will be contested at Cypress during the 2010 Olympics. And competitors in extreme skiing, where courses are set on ultimate ungroomed terrain, including cliffs and rocks, while not yet dignified by Olympic recognition, bear more than a passing resemblance to the downhill kamikazes from the early years of this century. The mythic heroes of the Jeldness Tea Party no doubt look on, perhaps slightly bemused by the new forms clothing these skills, but nodding in approval. We stand on the shoulders of these giants.

Military Rangers

Many Hollyburn skiers turned their outdoor talents to their country's protection during World War II. The Hollyburn Ridge Rangers was one of several companies formed in the aftermath of the Japanese attack on Pearl Harbor, which many feared was a precursor to a Japanese invasion of the mainland. Major Angus McAlister of Caulfeild was appointed, along with Reeve J. Edwards Sears, to command No. 2 Company Coast Defence Guards, Hollyburn Ridge Rangers, which was formed to protect West Vancouver from attack via Hollyburn Ridge. By July 1942 they numbered 173, divided into five detachments, with their headquarters at the Conservative Hall, later Sagers Maple Shop, and now the Dundarave Café and other businesses. They were outfitted in tree-green waterproof hats, ties, hunting coats, waterproof pants and khaki shirts to merge with the woodland areas.

Armed initially with wooden rifles, they were eventually equipped with 30-30 Winchester carbines and a few Sten guns. In target competitions they were more than a match for regular military personnel, perhaps because they paid for their own bullets. Fred Martin, who had served with the Gordon Highlanders during the Boer War, was

Hollyburn Rangers, early 1940s.
(HOLLYBURN HERITAGE SOCIETY ARCHIVES)

instrumental in setting up the rifle range high on the British Pacific Properties. An indoor practice gallery was also set up at the Garvin Ice and Fuel Plant. Their field headquarters was at Cypress Creek, about one mile west of the Hollyburn Ski Camp. Jim Piercy, ski club member, directed the ridge activity from Cabin "A" at the Hollyburn Ski Camp. During weekly sessions they were trained in a variety of military skills, including handling weapons, field craft, signalling, first aid, knots, living-off-the-land and map and compass reading. If an invasion occurred, they would be required to fight alongside regular troops.

While they never did see military action, they did help search for missing RCAF planes and Lend-Lease planes flying from the US to Russia via Alaska. On other occasions they acted as guides for regular forces in the BC bush. A stand-down ceremony was held in Brockton Oval on September 30, 1945. An honour guard from No. 1 Battalion of the King's Own Rifles of Canada presented arms as a final mark of respect for a job well done.

Select Bibliography

■ BOOKS

Ashburner, Tim. *The History of Ski Jumping*. Wykey, Shrewsbury, England: Quiller Press, 2003.

Bradbury, Elspeth. *A View Through the Trees*. District of West Vancouver, 2007.

Cannings, Richard and Sydney. *Geology of British Columbia: A Journey Through Time*. Vancouver: Greystone Books, 1999.

Haxthow, Eilif. "Hollyburn Journal" of 1924–1928. Trans. Jorgen Dahlie (unpublished).

Morley, Alan. *From Milltown to Metropolis*. Vancouver: Mitchell Press, 1974.

Nicol, Eric. *Vancouver*. Toronto: Doubleday, 1978.

Pojar, Jim and Andy MacKinnon, Comp. *Plants of Coastal British Columbia, Including Washington, Oregon & Alaska*. Vancouver: Lone Pine Publishing, 1994.

Ramsey, Bruce. *A Place of Excellence: A Chronicle of West Vancouver, 1912–1987*. Corporation of the District of West Vancouver, ca. 1986.

Ricker, Karl. "Hollyburn Ridge: A Snapshot of Its Historical Cabin Record." November 30, 1997 (unpublished).

Van Pelt, Robert. *Forest Giants of the Pacific Coast*. Vancouver: Global Forest Press, 2001.

Varner, Collin. *Plants of Vancouver and the Lower Mainland*. Vancouver: Raincoast Books, 2002.

Wormington, Stan. *The Ski Race*. Sandpoint, Idaho: Selkirk Press, 1980.

■ REPORTS

Alpine Outdoor Recreation Resources Limited. "Submission to District Forester Vancouver Forest District for permission to clear selected areas of the Valley Royal development," June 1966.

Alpine Outdoor Recreation Resources Limited. "A proposal for the establishment of a year-round multiple use Outdoor Recreational Development in the Cypress Bowl area," [1968].

"Amendment to Park use permit 1506," February 20, 2001.

BC Parks. "Cypress Park Master Plan," June 1997.

BC Parks. "Cypress Provincial Park: Draft Management Options," 1990.

BC Parks. "Master Plan background report for Cypress Provincial Park," April 1992.

Bufo Incorporated Sherlock Consulting. "Old Growth Park Strategy for Protection" (Draft), February 24, 2006.

"Cypress Bowl Recreations' Master Concept Plan." Public brief, March 1992.

"Cypress Old Growth Ecological Study." District of West Vancouver, October 31, 1991.

"Cypress Provincial Park Land Use Options: A Qualitative Analysis of Public Views." Viewpoints Research Ltd., August 1995.

"Environmental Assessment Report for the Cypress Venue," March 13, 2006.

Hollyburn Ridge Committee Report to Municipal Council, May 3, 1976.

Hollyburn Ridge Committee Report, March 1981.

"Hollyburn Ridge Golf Course." Technical/Environmental Feasibility Study. Talisman Land Resource Consultants, December 1989.

Jacques Whitford: Engineering, Scientific, Planning and Management Consultants. "Environmental Assessment Report for Cypress Mountain." Project no. BCV50473.

"Master Plan Background Report," April 1992.

Neill, John W. "The Proposed Hollyburn Ridge Golf Course." A report prepared for the municipality of West Vancouver, January 1973.

Oikos Ecological Consultants. "Cypress Old Growth Ecological Study," October 31, 1991.

"Report on the Mountain Bike Trails in West Vancouver." Prepared by the District of West Vancouver, November 15, 2000.

Sampson, Len. "What Went Wrong in Cypress Bowl: A Minority Report," September 1970.

Sinclair, James. "Report on the proposed creation and development of a park in the North Shore mountains," March 1939.

Turner, M.H. "The Concept for Cypress Provincial Park." Parks Branch, May 1976.

Williams, Bryan. "Report of the Cypress Park Special Planning Commission," August 1995.

Zirnhelt, Amber. "West Vancouver Mountain Bike Feasibility Study." August 2004.

■ NEWSLETTERS

The BC Mountaineer, 1923–1994.

BC Outdoors, 1984.

BC Skier, 1959, 1961.

The Bushwacker, 1938–1968.

The Cypress Bowl Mountaineer, 1994.

Cypress Log, 1945–1946.

Discovery (Vancouver Natural History Society), 1998–2003.

Hiker and Skier, 1933–1940.

Pioneer News (HSBC).

The Ridge Runner, 1979–2008.

Ski Trails, 1946–1960.

■ OTHER SIGNIFICANT SOURCES

Barrett, Dave (former B.C. premier)

CBC Vancouver (Marie-Helene Robitaille, Colin Preston).

District of West Vancouver Council Minutes

Grant, Don (Hollyburn Heritage Society)

Hollyburn Heritage Society Collection (West Vancouver Archives)

North Vancouver Archives

Rockandel, Catherine (Hollyburn Ridge Association)

Sinclair, James (papers in Special Collections, UBC)

Steig, Katharine (Friends of Cypress Provincial Park)

Swain, Bobby (Operations Manager, Cypress Bowl Ski Recreations Limited)

Swain, Linda (Manager, Cypress Bowl Ski Recreations Limited)

Taylor, Terry (Vancouver Natural History Society)

Index

Marquis Book Printing Inc.

Québec, Canada
2008